How the Hell Did I Not Know That?

HOW THE HELL DID I NOT KNOW THAT?

My Midlife Year from Couch to Curiosity

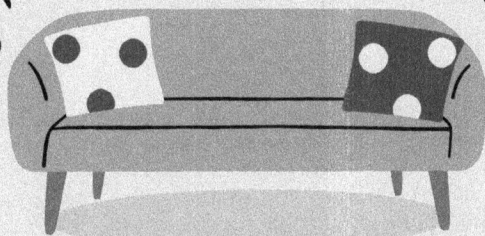

LUCIE FROST

Trinity University Press • San Antonio, Texas

Trinity University Press
San Antonio, Texas 78212

Names and identifying characteristics of some individuals who appear in
this book have been changed. Some dialogue has been recreated.

Book design by Anne Richmond Boston
Author photo by sRagnar Fotografi

Page 48, US beef cuts, courtesy Wikipedia Commons; page 51, photo by
author; page 67, golf ball dimples, by Prakul Varshney, courtesy Wikimedia Commons, CC BY-SA 4.0; page 144, braille alphabet, courtesy Mark
Skitsky/Shutterstock.com; page 148, phases of the moon, by Guy Vande-
grift, courtesy Wikimedia Commons, CC BY-SA 3.0; page 171, US map,
by Eric Pierce, courtesy Wikimedia Commons, CC BY-SA 3.0; page 174,
Calavera Catrina (Dapper Skeleton), ca. 1910, by José Guadalupe Posada,
courtesy Wikimedia Commons.

ISBN 978-1-59534-318-5 paper
ISBN 978-1-59534-317-8 ebook

Trinity University Press strives to produce its books using methods and
materials in an environmentally sensitive manner. We favor working
with manufacturers that practice sustainable management of all natural
resources, produce paper using recycled stock, and manage forests with
the best possible practices for people, biodiversity, and sustainability. The
press is a member of the Green Press Initiative, a nonprofit program ded-
icated to supporting publishers in their efforts to reduce their impacts on
endangered forests, climate change, and forest-dependent communities.

The paper used in this publication meets the minimum requirements of
the American National Standard for Information Sciences—Permanence
of Paper for Printed Library Materials, ansi 39.48–1992.

CIP data on file at the Library of Congress
29 28 27 26 25 | 5 4 3 2 1

Contents

For my brilliant, funny mother, Susan Toomey Frost,
who passed along her love for learning,
language, and humor

The best thing you can possibly do with your life is to tackle the motherfucking shit out of it.

— CHERYL STRAYED

!?

All the Days

In the month since I quit work, all I've done is watch *90 Day Fiancé*. Okay, okay, I'm exaggerating. I've also watched *90 Day Fiancé: Happily Ever After*, *90 Day Fiancé: Before the 90 Days*, and *90 Day Fiancé: What Now*. And, when I've gotten bored with the fiancé-ing, *Project Runway*, *America's Next Top Model*, and *Married at First Sight*.

I have no idea what day of the week it is. I wouldn't even know the time of day if it weren't for food. If I'm drinking coffee and eating toast, it's morning. A sandwich means lunchtime. Raw almonds, chocolate, tortilla chips, fruit, more chips, an upset stomach, where are the damn cashews?—that's afternoon. Flaky white fish, quinoa, and one glass of wine, well, maybe another glass of wine, and only one more really, except this little sip—those come in the evening.

Quick internet search: "Do retirees forget the day of the week?"

Oh good, there's an article on this in *Sixty and Me*, which likes to calls itself the "Largest Global Lifestyle Magazine for Dynamic Older Women."

I'm somewhat offended by their tagline. I can hear one marketing guy say, "Naw, I don't see this magazine being for all older women. Just the dynamic ones."

To which the other marketing guy says, "Do you think there are enough of them, though—of the dynamic ones—to sustain a whole magazine?"

The article, titled "Is Every Day Saturday When You Are Retired? 3 Ways to Keep Your Schedule Interesting," is even worse than the publication's tagline. I am sparing you the content beneath each subheading, because I'm nice that way:

"From Visiting the Doc to Everything Else"

"Volunteering at Local Organizations"

"Do Things Together"

What's with this bullshit advice *Sixty and Me* gives to us dynamic, older women? *Go to the doctor!* Nothing says "not Saturday" like a fun doctor outing! *Volunteer!* Did you never think of that before? So glad you read this article! *Do things!* Yes, do things!

I can't have gone from twenty-seven years as an employment lawyer to requiring doctors' appointments to know the day of the week.

"Remind me why I decided to retire early?" I said to my husband, Rob.

"Because you hated going to work every day and wanted to save the world?"

"I meant that rhetorically," I said, then switched from Hulu to Netflix.

Every day on my work commute, I listened to NPR stories about the government locking migrants in detention centers, climate change causing hurricanes and wildfires, and politicians being politicians. Then I parked my car, walked into the office, and spent my day managing workplace drama—like what to do about the technician who wrote "ASSHAT

PARKING!" in chalk behind the car of a coworker who did, in fact, park like a total asshat.

I knew I should be helping asylum seekers, working at the food bank, anything. But first I'd have to deal with the asshat parking situation.

"What led you to write something like that?" I asked the technician.

"He parked almost on top of my motorcycle, like an asshat," he said.

And then I talked to Asshat Parker, who helpfully explained, "He's the assclown."

Couldn't these guys come up with anything better than the fighting words of a twelve-year-old boy?

"Asswipe."

"No, you're the asswipe, assbag!"

"Who you calling an assbag, assface?"

This, while there were immigrant children sleeping in cells, separated from their parents, just two hours down the road. I just couldn't.

Not many people had the means to drop everything and make themselves useful in this world. I did, so how could I justify spending my days mediating ass insults?

But I couldn't make myself quit. What if I left my job and regretted it? I'd never find another job this good, if I could find one at all. As a woman over fifty, I'd be nearly unemployable. I'd have an aneurysm, survive but be incapacitated, blow through my retirement savings in one year, have my house foreclosed on, and somehow lose all of my front teeth—or worse yet, all but one of my front teeth.

I had to keep working for at least another five years, unless I was willing to do some major financial downsizing.

I decided a weekend in the redwoods would do me good. I had gotten a newsletter from Cheryl Strayed (who wrote

Tiny Beautiful Things, one of the best books on earth, and *Wild*, which is no slouch either) announcing that she and Elizabeth Gilbert (of *Eat, Pray, Love* fame) would be leading a workshop in California. The workshop, titled Brave Magic, promised to help you "mine your curiosity, support your creativity, and embrace your challenges with courage." It didn't sound too woo-woo, and I could use a little curiosity, creativity, and courage, so what the hell.

I got to the conference and walked into a ballroom of women—thirty-five- to forty-year-old artist types, each with a messy top bun, cat-eye reading glasses, a pashmina, a brightly colored journal, and a glitter pen. I had all the same things, but mine were off—hair (gray wash-and-wear ball of frizz), eyewear (plain old tortoise with smudged lenses), wrap (old airplane blanket), writing pad (Amazon Basics black-and-white composition notebook), ink (Bic ballpoint). I wasn't cool enough to be here.

Cheryl and Liz started off talking about being stuck in our lives and being afraid to address things we know need changing. They cautioned us not to search for the perfect solution, explaining (and this isn't an exact quote because I accidentally left my personal stenographer at home):

> Deep down, you know what you need. This is your Clarity talking to you, and you should trust that inner voice, embracing the truth in you more strongly than the fear in you. You can't get to any deeper truth or meaning in your life without being open to hearing the first truth. One truth leads to another, which leads to another. Your job is simply to put the key in the door.

Cheryl then asked us to get our pens. My seat neighbor pulled out her feathered stylus, which must have been a gift from a fairy. Mine came from Office Depot in a pack of seventy-two, seventy-five of which the kids swiped from my desk drawer within a week; then I had to borrow this one from my sixteen-year-old, who complained, "That's my only pen, Mom."

"Write down these words," Cheryl said. "This is your Clarity, and this is what I know about you."

When we were done writing, she said, "And now write a letter to yourself from your Clarity. Go! Write as much as you can as fast as you can, without thinking about what you're writing."

And this is what my Clarity had to say to me:

> Dear Lucie,
> This is your Clarity, and here is what I know about you. You are in your head, surviving on the energy of drama. You can't keep trying to fix everyone else's problems. Fix your own.
>
> Quit your job! Give as much notice as you feel you must, but Quit. Your. Job.
>
> It's scary. Do it anyway. If you have to sell your house, you can do that. But don't worry about that now. Take the first step. Quit. Your. Job.

Shit. My Clarity had me pegged, but why did it have to be such an insistent motherfucker?

Later that evening, I was back in my room at the retreat center, three glasses into a bottle of cabernet. My drunk brain said, "You know what? Clarity was kind of an asshole, but it was also kind of right. You need to quit your job. In fact, do it now—right now!—before you have a chance to change your mind."

The wee bit sober part of my brain said, "Shouldn't you think about it? Maybe talk it over with Rob first?"

"Nope," Drunk Brain said. "Trust your Clarity."

High on conference energy and cabernet, Drunk Brain sent this text to my boss:

> Hey, I have so, so much respect for you. And I'm oddly, almost creepily, or absolutely fan girly anyway, in awe of you. *{Career advice: Never start your resignation letter with the word "Hey." It just seems, I dunno, unprofessional? Also, never use the word "creepily" in a note to your boss, even if tempered by the word "almost." It just seems, I dunno, super duper creepy?}* And I so, so want you to succeed—in whatever success means to you. I love how you talk about how many times you have been married. And how much of a bust those marriages have been. And how much you love your husband. And how long it may take him to finish the bathroom remodel. And how much you love that about him. *{Jesus Christ, put down that iPhone! What are you doing? Do not continue!}* And I love how very honest and vulnerable, and brilliant and awkward you are. And . . . *{I said ABORT! Do you not listen? She's the awkward one? Put that damn phone down!}* I've got to quit. And I couldn't have any more respect for you, and couldn't be any more in your camp, but I've got to go. *{Okay, that's enough now, sweetie. Set the phone on the bed and*

rest your head on the pillow. Get a good night's sleep. If you still want to send the text in the morning, I promise I'll let you.} And I'll give you all of the time you need, but I'm having headaches and chest pains. And remember how I said I didn't think I'd have migraines on a beach in Mexico? I also don't think I'd have chest tightness at my townhome in San Antonio. *{Sigh.}*

So let's talk. Not urgently but earnestly. And I'm going to send this before I have a chance to second-guess myself and EEK! Let's talk. *{Great work, Lucie. That was a super classy way to end your career. Brava.}*

So yeah, that's how I ended up sitting here on my couch, streaming reality TV shows. Yes, my plan was to retire and spend my days offering up my services at the nearest immigrant detention center, but as it turns out I am incapable of having a conversation with another person, venturing out of the house, or putting my big bosoms in a bra. *{Not bragging. They're more long than they are big, really.}*

Last night I dreamed I bought a house. It was my first day there, so I wandered around, trying to find my way through the place. I opened a door and discovered an extra bedroom.

"That's nice," I thought. "This will make a comfortable office."

Then I opened what I thought was a closet door, only to find a hallway. As I walked through, I realized the house had another wing.

Another door led to gardens. The gardens led to a turret. The turret's circular staircase led to a large room housing fifteen people, all now in my employ.

All the Days

Back in the house I found more hidden rooms, floors, attics, statues, furnishings, and on and on, in various states of disrepair.

I came across a wine bottle. Thank God! I took a swig, then dangled the bottle by my side as I wandered on, discovering additional responsibilities behind every door. I got more and more drunk and my hair became more and more disheveled, until I collapsed in tears on the parquet floor of an art gallery I stumbled upon.

You who are psychologists can tell me what this dream really means. I interpret it like this: I feel overwhelmed. I don't know what's coming next in my life, what's behind the next door, and I'm terrified. Up to now, my life has been a neat progression. I raised my hand, I answered the questions right, I became the teacher's pet, I got good grades, I got promoted grade to grade, I went to college, I graduated, I worked for a few years, I went to law school, I got a law job, I billed hours and more hours and more still.

But now? I can spend my days however I want, and my dreams are warning me that if I don't put some order in my life, if I don't figure out my life's floor plan, I'm going to end up alone in an art gallery hugging an empty bottle of hooch.

Because *90 Day Fiancé* hasn't aired an episode telling me what to do with my life, I don't know where to begin.

I could start joining groups, so I'd have to be social and connect with people. I could go on Meetup and find people with similar interests—which would have to be other people who want to stay in their houses, sit on their couches, and watch reality television. Basically, a Meetup group of folks who refuse to meet up.

This idea seems flawed.

I could make myself exercise every day. I could wake up early, put on leggings and a sports bra, and get outside while the day is new. I could walk the neighborhood streets, waving at folks as I go by.

And that shit ain't never gonna happen. Next!

What if I try learning my way out of this? Learning has always been my thing. I was one of those annoying kids in school who had the teacher saying, "Does anyone other than Lucie want to take a shot at the answer?" I was the college kid who was hella fun but still made sure her GPA didn't dip below a 4.0. I was the law school student who played it cool after they posted grades but was secretly smug when another student walked up and said, "Oh, wow, Lucie. I had no idea you were one of the smart ones."

What if I acknowledge that, for right now, I am not in a position to do anything but watch television? What if I allow myself to do that, but only if I am learning while I'm watching?

That's it.

While I'm watching TV, I'm going to put my key in the door of curiosity by noticing any little thing I'd like to know more about. I'll read up and learn about it. And then I'll learn about the next bit of something I'm curious about. And the next.

When I'm up for it, I'll expand from television to something else. Maybe I can learn about something in another room or down the block. I'll inch my way out in the world by learning about things I'm curious about—any simple thing I didn't already know.

I will *brain* my way out of this. I will follow every curiosity and see where it leads me. I'll discover what fascinates me. And the best thing? I get to start on the couch! Project Couch to Curiosity!

How perfect will my research into each curiosity need to be?

Perfect enough to satisfy the curiosity.

Will I use good sources?

I'll allow myself to go heavier on Wikipedia than I would if I were writing a research paper. How does a goal of 76 to 91 percent accuracy sound?

Writing about what I learn will make me feel useful again, a little bit like I have a job—a mission to teach you all of the things I have learned. It will keep me busy, provide structure to my days, and distract me from online shopping. And hopefully it will connect me with real, live people I can learn from and with.

You, Friend I Probably Haven't Met Yet but Can't Wait to Meet Because You're Great Fun I'm Sure, might be wondering what's in it for you. Well, you'll learn things you never thought to wonder about, in a way that I hope is more entertaining and less time-consuming than digging around on your own (and if you didn't wonder about the things because you already knew them, I suppose you'll get to feel superior, which, yay!). Who knows, maybe you'll be inspired to get off the couch and start chasing your own curiosities.

And when my curiosities are researched and this book is done, one marketing guy will ask, "Is it for the dynamic, older woman?"

And I'll say, "It's for all women—but probably older ones with time to explore things they're curious about."

And he'll say, "But are there enough curious women to sustain a whole book?"

And I'll say, "Fuck you. Just fuck you."

All the Television

I'm starting this new venture with learning about television. I get to watch the same shows I'm already watching—all the *90 Day Fiancés*—but add some learning. Baby steps, people. Sure, it would be nice if I'd tune into PBS once in a while, but my brain is healing from a lifetime of working. It needs a minute.

Did I think I'd be spending my retirement learning factoids from reality television? No, I did not. When I fantasized about retiring, I imagined I would wake up early for a daily run, say 6:30 a.m., to beat the heat. I'd get home, do some meditating and journaling, eat a healthy breakfast, and enjoy my morning reading. I'd get together with girlfriends for lunch, then solve world problems between 2 and 5 p.m.—maybe sorting cans at the food bank, delivering meals to the elderly, or fixing the pesky climate crisis. My husband and I would cook dinner together (never mind that I don't know how to cook—this is a fantasy, people!), and I would drink a single glass of wine (again, a fantasy). We'd retire to the bedroom early (y'know, more fantasy).

The reality: I wake up around 9 a.m. I wear exercise clothes, though there's not a chance in hell I'm stepping outdoors. It's just Too. Damn. Hot. And I'm Too. Damn. Lazy. I make coffee and a slice of toast, sit on the couch, and stay there for the day. If the phone rings I don't answer, because how important could it be? Besides, I'm watching *90 Day Fiancé*, I'm in the middle of a season, and I have to know why Mohamed is saying that Danielle's hoo-ha smells. At about 3 p.m. I get sleepy, so I take a nap, just to make sure it'll be a struggle to sleep at night. I wake at 5 p.m., eat whatever Rob hands me, and turn on the TV. I watch until bedtime while drinking a few glasses of wine. I care about sleep health, so when I wake up at 3 a.m., I do something soothing like doom-scroll. I fall asleep around 5 or 6 a.m., then restart the cycle.

Rob suggested I might need professional help working through this life transition. I know he is right. But I hate appointments with a new therapist because there's so much debriefing required before you can get to the good stuff.

"So, Lucie, how many children do you have?" the therapist would ask.

Ugh. Now I'd have to *share*, as if getting out of the house wasn't task enough.

"I have one husband—Rob—and three children. One out of college, that's Thomas, one in college, Mackenzie, and one a year from starting college, Clark. One stepdaughter, Kayla, who will start college next year. No abortions. No miscarriages. A Big Law job for seventeen years. Divorced from first husband. Spiraled. Quit work. Opened a ladies' boutique with a friend. Remarried to Rob. Decided I was ready to go back to law. There for seven years. Kids in cages. Climate crisis. Damn politicians. Asshat parking. Oddly, almost creepily, or absolutely fan girly anyway, in awe of my boss. Cringy text. *90 Day Fiancé.* And here I am."

"Well, we've got a lot to unpack then," the therapist would say.

I just can't bear having that conversation right now. So yes, I should see a therapist. But first I'm learning about television.

What do I hope to learn? I'm not going for quantum mechanics or Mandarin, just something that fires the synapses. Actually, "fires" is too big an expectation. Any little spark of curiosity will do.

Will You Marry Me?

Project Couch to Curiosity is meeting me where I am, and where I am is watching *90 Day Fiancé*—every season, every spinoff, and all of the happily-ever-afters.

The premise of *90 Day Fiancé* is this: an American and a non-American want to get married and live in the United States. The couple gets engaged, and the non-American applies for a K-1 fiancé(e) visa and moves to the United States. The couple must marry within ninety days.

Sounds easy, right? Wrong, wrong, wrong. Why? Because often the non-American is a scammer, and the American denies it and denies it until she's sitting in a dark kitchen with the electricity cut off, her bank account drained, and cat urine covering the floor. Or maybe the American is a god-awful-nightmare-of-a-human, and the foreigner has to decide whether it's really worth it to marry an asshole for the passport. Or they're both good, honest people, but once they live together they realize they like the same side of the bed, different news channels, or some other stranger they met on the internet. There are so many ways things can go astray, making for great television.

So here's the curiosity I have: Why do the couples get married in the United States instead of marrying abroad and then coming over? Is it easier to bring a fiancé(e) into the country than it is to bring a spouse?

My less than perfect research tells me yes and no.

Let's say you're a forty-five-year-old American woman named Tammy. You live in Arkansas and have five kids and mounds of debt. Where are you going to meet a guy in Arkansas willing to spend Saturday nights at the smoky bingo hall? So you hop on the internet, and within moments you meet Ahmed, a twenty-five-year-old dreamboat from Tunisia with rock hard abs and an angular jaw. Obviously it's the perfect match, and you fall deeply in love. The two of you decide you must be together forever, so you will marry and live your lives together in Arkansas. But how do you go about getting your Tunisian hunk over to the United States for the nuptials?

Option 1: The K-1 fiancé(e) visa. You could file for a K-1 visa, but first you have to meet Ahmed in person. You ask your best friend from high school to watch the kids so you and Ahmed can meet for a lovely vacation in Spain. You open up another credit card account and buy the ticket. You spend a week together in Madrid, drinking sangria and making sweet, sweet love.

When you get back to Arkansas, you're desperate to bring Ahmed home and show him off to your girlfriends, so you file the form to start the K-1 visa process. You submit proof that you have met in person within the prior two years—the Madrid vacation photos will do nicely, along with the hotel bill, your flight confirmation, maybe even the Trojan you saved from the first night he rocked your world. You submit proof that your relationship is legit—perhaps the transcripts from your long chat sessions, copies of the little sweet nothings he's mailed to you, and sworn statements from your friends attesting that you've lost your ever-lovin' mind and really are in love with this guy. You submit proof that you are above the poverty line, presumably showing that you can afford to support Ahmed until the wedding.

For his part, Ahmed submits police clearance from everywhere he's lived and a sealed medical exam. He has an interview at the US embassy nearest him, during which he proclaims his love for you and confirms he knows your middle name (Faye), your favorite soda (Orange Crush), and the shape of all of your birthmarks (oddly geometric).

Having convinced the powers that be of the genuineness of your relationship, the K-1 visa is approved in about seven months.

You fly Ahmed to Arkansas and begin to plan the wedding. You decide to invite cousin Ashley, even though she said Ahmed was "slicker than owl shit." You have the wedding in one month, which is within the required ninety-day window from visa approval. Ahmed then applies for the coveted green card and gets it about four months later.

The whole process—from the first application to the green card—costs you about $2,000 (plus whatever dough you spent on Madrid, Ahmed's flight, and the two-carat engagement ring you bought for a steal from Ahmed's third cousin's third cousin) and took about a year. Of those, you were only apart from Ahmed for the first seven months, since he was able to come to Arkansas right after the K-1 approval.

Option 2: The spousal visa. What if you marry Ahmed first instead, before bringing him to Arkansas? You dump your kids on your best friend, jump on a flight to Tunisia, fall into Ahmed's arms, and tie the knot.

You've got to get back for your next shift at Kroger, but sadly you can't bring Ahmed with you. He has to wait until he gets all of the required paperwork (medical exam, etc.) completed and the visa is approved, and that will take ten to thirteen months.

The spousal visa will only cost you about $1,200 though, quite a bit less than if you had gone the fiancé(e) visa route. Besides, once the visa is approved, Ahmed will immediately have a green card and can start working as soon as the plane touches down in the United States, so you can tell your boss Danny to "shove it up his big-boss asshole" once Ahmed's visa comes through. If the visa comes through, that is. You're screwed if you've done married the guy and the visa gets denied. But you're in love, so there's no room for such negative thinking.

Which option is better? It would seem the less expensive spousal visa is the way to go, if you can bear being apart for just a few more months. But here's the kicker. With the fiancé(e) visa, you promise to support Ahmed until you get married. What if you don't support him, because you spent your savings on box wine, lottery tickets, and nicotine patches? Nothing. You won't go to jail or owe him back pay.

With the spousal visa, you basically become Ahmed's financial sponsor until he dies or becomes a US citizen. If he uses certain public benefits, the government can (and will!) come after you to repay them even if he ditched you to run off with Tiffany, a stripper who also happens to be your ex-husband's sister.

This is the important lesson I wouldn't have known but for the time retirement has given me to focus on learning: If you end up falling in love with a twenty-five-year-old foreigner in a chat room, whatever you do, don't marry the dude, no matter how angular the jaw.

Do You Have the Clap?
Ahmed will need a medical exam to get his fiancé or spousal visa. But what health conditions will disqualify him?

It's a shorter list than you'd think:

- Communicable diseases. Like TB, leprosy, syphilis, and gonorrhea. *{I had to look up how to spell gonorrhea, which I guess is a good sign?}*
- Quarantinable diseases. Cholera, the plague, and the like. *{What is the plague anyway? I'll check into that and get back to you shortly.}*
- Current public health emergency stuff. Polio, smallpox, etcetera.
- Mental illness, with harm to yourself or others.
- History of drug abuse or addiction.

Cancer? Not a problem. I suppose the concern isn't about the public burden of treating an ailment but rather protecting others from catching it. Seems fair to me.

What the Hell Is the Plague?
Now that I know the plague would keep Ahmed from joining Tammy, I wonder what it is. A specific disease? Or an effect (like if it kills x number of people, we call it a plague)? Or perhaps it's a nickname we apply to various mass-killing diseases?

The plague is one specific type of bacterial infection—from *Yersinia pestis*—which is usually transmitted to humans through fleas. Another reason not to have dogs—except I love my sweet Labrador, Miley, so I'll have to take the risk.

The plague is still around, mostly in Africa, Asia, and South America, with only a few cases in the United States every year. Fortunately, it is treatable with antibiotics.

There are different types of plague, but those just refer to how you got the bacteria in you:

- Bubonic. Usually comes from an infected rodent or flea bite and goes into your lymphatic system. Bubonic plagues are characterized by swollen lymph nodes in the armpit or groin (called "buboes," deriving from the Greek word for groin).

- Septicemic. Travels from the lymphatic system into your blood stream. Septicemic plague is gonna kill you, and likely within twenty-four hours of first symptoms. Eek!
- Pneumonic. In your lungs, likely because some snotty-nosed kid sneezed or coughed on you. Another reason not to have another kid (as if your list of reasons wasn't already plenty lengthy).

There are other ways to get the plague, but I've reached my science limit. Like with everything, I learn just enough to satisfy my curiosity. If your curiosity is more particular about information, go get your own flea bites and write a research paper about what happens to you. But then don't complain that you don't have time to watch *90 Day Fiancé*.

Downton Abbey

I need a palate cleanser—a show that makes me feel a wee bit less pathetic than *90 Day Fiancé*—so I've chosen *Downton Abbey*.

If you watch *Downton*, you must be prepared. There will be words you don't understand—and that will be all of them if you forget to turn on closed-captioning. But even if you are able to simultaneously read the mush the Crawleys are speaking, there will be words you just don't know—unless you're a British aristocrat, I suppose, but then shouldn't you be off queening instead of reading this book? That's why you should keep Merriam-Webster by your side as you watch, so you can look up words like these:

Termagant: An overbearing or nagging woman; shrew.

Doughty: Marked by fearless resolution; valiant.

Chivvy: To tease or annoy with persistent petty attacks.

Suet: The hard fat about the kidneys and loins in beef and mutton that yields tallow.

Tallow: The white, nearly tasteless, solid rendered fat of cattle and sheep used chiefly in soap, candles, and lubricants.

Sadly, Merriam won't be able to help you with historical references—ones you should know but, if you're like me, don't. It's best to have Britannica by your side as well. The online version will have to do, since Britannica quit printing the bound sets in 2012 (and quit selling door-to-door way back in 1996).

You'll need Britannica to remind you of things like who Guy Fawkes is. You know there's a Guy Fawkes Day, of course, but you don't remember who the dude is because you daydreamed your way through history class. *{If I recall correctly, you were fantasizing about blue-eyed Edward, whom you wrote notes to—notes he wisely did not acknowledge receiving. But you kept writing them anyway because, to put it gently, you were a total weirdo. Oh, that wasn't you? Well, it definitely wasn't me who did that. Nope.}*

So I don't leave you wondering, Guy Fawkes was one of the Catholic conspirators who decided to blow up the House of Lords in 1605, with the goal of killing King James I and putting a Catholic monarch on the throne. The attempt, dubbed the Gunpowder Plot, was foiled when the authorities were tipped off by an anonymous letter. The conspirators were caught, and Fawkes (who was found guarding the explosives) was executed. Now UK folks celebrate the foiled attempt by lighting bonfires throughout the city.

These days when the parliamentary session opens with the king's or queen's speech, there is a nod to Guy Fawkes. The monarch's traditional bodyguards, called the Yeomen of the Guard, search the cellars for gunpowder. It's more of a costumed walk-through than a real search though, because the antiterror team handles security.

You'll also learn from *Downton* that during World War I you could be shot for cowardice—yet another reason I won't join the military right now, apart from being too old, weighing too much, and being incapable of climbing a rope. If someone were to point a gun at me, I'd start crying, empty my wallet, and offer up my firstborn (or maybe my second?). If I do get called to war somehow, they should just go ahead and shoot me at the start. I'd never survive in the military (so extra thanks to all of you who serve!).

By the way, the Wikipedia entry for cowardice reads, "See also: anxiety, fear, sissy, pussy, virtue, weakness." Sissy? Pussy? Seriously? Hey, Wikipedia, get with the times!

She Runs the Show

I pulled my eyes away from the TV screen long enough to check my email. Now that I don't need email to delegate undesirable job tasks, I don't have a sense of urgency about email. Yes, I could miss an Anthropologie sale, but they'll have four more of those next week.

I found another ad for MasterClass in my inbox. The MasterClass folks must know their online-learning program is exactly the sort of thing I'll buy if they're just persistent enough. They shoot ads for their video courses at me as if they were owls delivering Hogwarts invites.

Why would I love MasterClass? Well, it's

1. learning
2. you can do from your couch
3. with celebrities

If they had gotten some TV star to teach my history classes (especially one as dreamy as blue-eyed Edward), maybe I'd know something.

This ad was for Shonda Rhimes's class. I know she's the showrunner for about every show on television, but I don't know what a showrunner is.

Obviously, the showrunner runs the show, but is she the director? Producer? Head writer? What exactly?

A showrunner is the executive producer of the television show—the real executive producer, not an executive producer credited because she came up with funding for the show, has a big name that'll help sell it, or is a bratty lead actor who threatened to quit if her name wasn't in the credits in capital letters. The showrunner manages and has creative authority over the show and is answerable only to the network. The showrunner is in charge of the writers, the crew, the budget, everything.

Now there's a job I wouldn't want.

Do you know what television job I would want? Writer would be nice, of course, but assuming that job was taken, food stylist. It's an actual job—one that gives you pay and probably benefits too.

What does a food stylist do? In a scene where food is particularly important, the food stylist "casts" the food and ensures that all of the food details are historically and geographically accurate. The stylist makes sure the food looks yummy, lasts or is replaced for the day's filming, and is palatable to the actors.

Movie and television food stylists have a harder job than magazine food stylists. For movies and television, most of the food needs to be edible (and stay edible through a long day of filming) so actors don't accidentally get poisoned. The stylists have to think about the smells of the foods and about the actors' food allergies and preferences. *{Don't you know food stylists are so annoyed by picky eaters and vegans? We all are, I suppose.}* They also have to ensure that the food looks good from any camera angle (directors usually prefer real food for this reason) and that it is perfect for every take (because there's no telling which take will be used).

For magazines, the photographer is taking still shots, which are more forgiving. The stylist can make a slew of fairly good-looking dishes for the setup shots and then bring in the hero/beauty dish when the photographer is ready to start shooting the real thing. The stylist can make ice cream out of mashed potatoes, milk out of Elmer's glue, or brownies out of a toddler's diaper contents, provided they look real.

If movie and television food stylists are responsible for cooking edible food, I've got a problem. Cooking is a skill I don't have. How unskilled am I as a cook? I made breakfast for my oldest son, Thomas, when he was five or six.

"Mommy, this is so good. What do they call this?" he said.

"Toast, honey. They call it toast."

So that food stylist job? Never mind. I quit.

I Will Survive

Speaking of Thomas, he came to town and I told him about Project Couch to Curiosity. He sounded excited but a bit confused. "Couldn't you just enjoy your retirement without having to make it a project?"

"Well, sure, I could, but apparently I can't."

"Whatever," he said. He's a live-and-let-live type.

Poor Thomas. I call him my training child, because I practiced all my inflexible rules on him, then decided life would be happier for all of us if I tossed the rules out for kids two and three.

Thomas graduated from college a few years back and in his free time is busying himself watching every season of *Survivor*. Some of your kids may be researching disease-prevention solutions for developing countries, but remember, Thomas is my spawn. Of course he's watching every season of *Survivor*.

I'm curious: Do people really still watch that show?

Survivor has been airing since 2000, and though ratings have gone down over the years it's still a solid performer. Back in season two, it averaged 29.8 million viewers an episode. Now it's down to about 7.5 million, but that still puts it in the top twenty-five most-watched TV shows.

Survivor has filmed in twenty-one locations over all the years but made Fiji its permanent location in 2016. Fiji provides a rebate for filming costs to the show, rumored to be about 45 percent.

A few interesting rules for *Survivor* contestants:

> No quid pro quo (e.g., offering someone money for immunity)
> No agreeing to share a prize
> No going over to the other team's camp without producer permission
> No sitting out on a challenge or tribal council
> No refusing to vote at tribal council
> No voting for yourself at tribal council

> No withholding illness or symptoms from the
> medical team
> No stealing food

Would I survive on *Survivor*? For about three days. After that, hunger and dehydration would cause migraines to kick in, and there's no television show worth migraines.

Collapse Those Shoulders

I was telling my friend Liz about everything I've been doing since I retired—watching TV, the telly, the idiot box, the boob tube, and then there's the small screen.

"Why so much TV?" Liz said.

"I dunno. This retirement thing is throwing me for a loop, I guess, and TV seems a better escape than heroin."

I thought later about why retirement has been so disorienting. There are things about work I didn't anticipate missing—structure to my day, being around people, being helpful. And I didn't realize how much of my identity was tied up in work. Every time someone asks me what I do, I have no answer for them.

"What do I do? Nothing. Absolutely nothing."

Thinking about that makes my brain hurt. But you know what? It's *Project Runway* time again! That's what I do! I learn things about *Project Runway*.

In this first episode, they assigned the designers their workspaces and mannequins. I noticed a mannequin marked "Collapsible Shoulder."

What is that? Obviously, the shoulders of the mannequin collapse, but how and why?

Answer: With a collapsible shoulder dress form, you can push each of the shoulders in about four inches, so you can easily pull tight-fitting garments off the form.

It would be convenient if my shoulders could collapse. Even better? Collapsible inner thighs.

Love Me Tenter

Doing this project, I'm noticing things that I thought I was right about but wasn't. It's not that I think I know everything, but I'm discovering that I don't know even the things I do know.

I had closed-captioning on for *Downton Abbey* (which again, is the only way to watch the show and make any sense of it), and I discovered the word is not "tenderhooks" but "tenterhooks." How the hell did I not know that?

A tenter is a frame with hooks that holds and stretches fabric taut for drying. The word comes from the Latin word *tentōrium*, meaning a tent.

When you're on tenterhooks, you're being stretched tensely, like the fabric.

That reminds me of the time I got in trouble for affixing my Slinky to the antenna of the TV and walking backward, stretching the Slinky until Chester tipped over, crashing the TV to the ground.

Who is Chester, you ask? Chester Drawers, of course.

Lost in His Eyes

I'm watching CNN now. You might think this is a step forward from reality TV. You might be wrong. Instead of listening to the news and being world-informed, I'm wondering if Anderson Cooper's eyes are really that blue. Is he wearing colored contacts?

The internet tells me, "They're that blue. Plus, I have a rabbit hole you might like to go down."

"Sure!" I say.

Did you know Anderson Cooper sunburned his eyes once?

I didn't even know that was a thing. It's called photokeratitis, which is caused by overexposure to UV rays.

After a day filming in Portugal with the sun reflecting off the water, Cooper woke in the night with his eyes afire (not literally, of course, though that's a fun visual). He went blind for thirty-six hours.

Photokeratitis most often happens during skiing. Snow blindness.

How the hell did I not know that's what snow blindness is? I thought it was when it's snowing so hard you can't see. Good grief.

This One's for You, Rob

Rob likes that I'm learning new things—not so much for me, I suspect, but because it benefits him. He sends me quick texts of things he doesn't know and is too lazy to look up, hoping I am not too lazy to look them up.

Last evening's text said just this, which I'm guessing must have come up from a *Downton* episode: "Small beer. And almoner, of the hospital."

So Rob, this one's for you, from your information concierge:

> **Small beer:** Weak or crappy beer, but also something weak or trivial.
> **Almoner:** The term historically referred to anyone (though usually a church official) responsible for dispensing alms—food or money given to the needy. In the hospital context, it originally referred to the person responsible for determining whether patients qualified for indigent assistance. Over time the hospital almoner role expanded to responsibility for patient welfare and aftercare

and ultimately evolved into the hospital social worker position.

Cross Your Heart

Rob mentioned that Mariska Hargitay (of *Law & Order* fame) is the daughter of old-timey actress Jayne Mansfield. He asked if I remembered Jayne Mansfield.

"Sure, she was the bra lady," I said.

"The bra lady?"

"You know, from the Cross Your Heart commercials."

"Oh, that's another Jane," Rob said. "Jane Russell did the Howard Hughes Cross Your Heart commercials."

"Wait, what? Howard Hughes?"

"Yeah, he invented the Cross Your Heart bra."

"Really?"

"Cross my heart."

Is that true? I hate to fact-check Rob (yeah, right), but for the Couch to Curiosity cause . . .

I'm glad Rob didn't hope to die, because he's wrong.

Howard Hughes directed *The Outlaw*, starring Jane Russell in her first film role. When Hughes saw the dailies for the movie, he was disappointed with the look of Russell's bosom, so he designed an underwire push-up bra for her. In her autobiography she confessed that she found Hughes's bra uncomfortable, so unbeknownst to him she wore her tired old bra during filming and stuffed the cups with tissue.

Russell would go on to become one of the leading Hollywood sex symbols of the 1940s and 1950s. She played alongside Marilyn Monroe in *Gentlemen Prefer Blondes* and allegedly tried to convert Monroe to Christianity during filming, unsuccessfully. At the age of eighty-two, Russell described herself to the *Daily Mail* as "a teetotal, mean-spirited, right-wing, narrow-minded, conservative Christian bigot, but not a racist." Charming.

Anyhow, Hughes's bra has nothing to do with the Cross Your Heart bra, which was invented by Playtex. Being of ample bosom, Russell was cast in the Playtex commercials hawking a bra she actually did find comfortable.

And now, steel yourself because your mind is about to be blown (unless you already know what I'm about to tell you, in which case it won't be blown at all, but you can experience the joy of seeing other people's minds blown).

Do you know who invented the hook-and-eye bra clasp? Samuel Clemens, also known as Mark Fucking Twain. Damn, I bet Howard Hughes would have been livid if he knew Mark Twain was the one holding up Jane Russell's mighty bosom.

!?

All the Food and Drink

I'm ready to expand my learning beyond television. It might be tricky, because the couch has a magnetic force. I try to get up to do something, but its power is too strong. It slams me back on my behind, and there I am, searching what other countries and regions have *Next Top Model* series. *{About all of them: Africa, Albania, Australia, Austria, Belgium, Benelux, Brazil, Canada, the Caribbean, China, Colombia, Croatia, Denmark, Estonia, the Far East, Finland, France, Germany, Greece, Hungary, India, Indonesia, Israel, Italy, Mexico, Mongolia, the Netherlands, New Zealand, Norway, Peru, Philippines, Poland, Romania, Russia, Scandinavia, Serbia, Slovakia, Slovenia, South Korea, Sweden, Switzerland, Thailand, Turkey, Ukraine, United Kingdom, United States, Vietnam. Dang, that's quite a fierce empire Tyra has built.}*

Here's what I know. There are only two things in nature strong enough to overcome the couch's force field: food and booze. It's possible that Marie Curie discovered their demagnetizing properties. I'm not sure.

Those of you who retired before I did have likely discovered that the love of food and drink can be tricky math during retirement. Here's the calculus:

- No work = No money.
- No money = Fuck it, let's go to the restaurant anyway.
- Let's go to the restaurant anyway = Big credit card bill.
- Big credit card bill + no income to pay it = Oops!

Or this one:

- No work = No need to wake up early.
- No need to wake up early = Just one more glass of wine.
- Just one more glass of wine × seven nights = Just a few more pounds.
- Just one more glass of wine × one hundred nights = Well, now we have a problem, don't we?

A mighty alcohol problem (to which I'm mighty prone) isn't part of the retirement fantasy. Hence, this phase of Project Couch to Curiosity: food/booze learning, plus a wee bit of caution.

Bone the Branzino
I'm still not ready for venturing outside the walls of my house. To keep with the spirit of the project, I'm going to learn things about others' food and drink experiences. Is that cheating? Let's say no.

"The waiter boned the branzino tableside," Rob reported after coming home from dinner with his friend Matthew.

"In public? Isn't that illegal?" I said.

"Isn't what illegal?"

"Boning a fish, and in public no less. I think you meant debone."

"No, the word is 'bone.' Like 'I bone the chicken.'"

"Rob, boning means boinking."

Rob insisted the proper word is "bone." I headed to my favorite grammar website, Grammarist, to prove him wrong.

> Bone, when used as a verb, means to remove the *bones* from meat or fish, usually before cooking. . . . Debone means to remove the *bones* from meat or fish, usually before cooking.

What, Grammarist? I can leave aside that you put the word "bones" in italics for no apparent reason. But those two definitions are the same damn thing! You are not helping me win the debate with my husband. Now I have to go to Urban Dictionary, and God only knows what sort of filth I'll find there.

Bone
1. (v) To have sexual intercourse. "Your aim is to bone" — Tribe Called Quest
2. (n) Penis. "You can act like a doggy, and play with my bone" — Schoolly

Debone
A verb that can be used as a substitute for wank. "I can't slip you one now, I deboned 20 minutes ago." #wank #handshandy #flog #rubout #grateacarrot

You see, Grammarist? Filth, and for nothing, because it didn't let me prove to Rob that it's not right to bone the branzino tableside. Worse yet, you left me stuck with the carrot-grating visual.

After spending far too much time looking at dictionaries and cooking sites, I discovered that Rob was right. While both bone and debone work, bone is the preferred term. But shhhhh, can we keep this just between us so he doesn't get too big an ego? *{It'll also make a great way to test whether Rob really reads this book. If he never boasts about having been right, he'll be busted for not even making it to the third chapter.}*

Pee on an Egg
More learning about food from the comfort of my couch. I read a tweet suggesting you can unboil an egg with urine. Three questions:

 1. Huh?
 2. Can you really unboil an egg?
 3. With urine?

Yes, you can unboil an egg. The white and the yolk of an egg are each made up of folded protein strands. When you heat them, the molecules bounce around, the proteins unfold, the white and yolk proteins bond together, and you get a squishy cooked egg. The trick to unboiling the egg is to get the proteins to fold up again.

Add urea, an ingredient found in urine. This liquifies the egg white. Then you can spin the yolk and liquified white in your vortex spinner, and voilà! The proteins fold back up and you've got yourself an unboiled egg. *{What? You don't have a vortex spinner? Did you give it away when you purged your ice cream maker, your vegetable juicer, and your first husband?}*

But why, oh why, oh why?

The scientists who made this unboil an egg discovery won the 2015 Ig Nobel Prize in Chemistry. The Ig Nobel is a parody of the Nobel Prize. It is awarded to "honor achievements that first make people laugh and then make them think." At first, unboiling an egg sounds funny. Ha! But the discovery has numerous important applications, including for improved delivery of targeted cancer treatment drugs, which then makes you think, doesn't it?

You could probably spend your entire retirement reading about the Ig Nobel winners. Here's a taste of the 2002 awards to give you a feel (I happened to land on that year when I spotted the phrase "scrotal asymmetry").

- **Medicine:** Awarded to a scientist who wrote a paper on scrotal asymmetry, which concluded that in men, the right testicle is higher and larger than the left; and that in Greek statues, the right testicle is correctly portrayed as higher but incorrectly portrayed as smaller than the left. The thinking is that the Greeks must have assumed that the left testicle, being lower, was the heavier and larger of the two. *{Oh, now you're curious about why men's penises are always so small in Greek statues? How weird! Me too. Turns out it's because Greek statues represented the ideal man, and back in those days, large penises were not considered ideal, instead being associated with unathleticism and stupidity.}*
- **Biology:** Awarded to a team who discovered that ostriches were failing to mate because of the presence of humans. The ostriches had begun to court their human handlers, rather than getting frisky with their own. *{Of all the animals I would want sexually attracted to me, ostriches have to be at the bottom. Of the list, I mean.}*
- **Peace:** Awarded to a company that invented Bow-Lingual, a computer-based automatic dog-to-human translation device, for promoting peace among the species. The wireless device analyzes dog barks, categorizes them into one of six emotional categories (happy, sad, frustrated, on guard, assertive, and needy) and displays phrases associated with each category. *{I'd*

have no need to categorize my dog Miley's barks, because they'd be needy, needy, needy, needy, needy, and needy. Hell, my barks would probably be the same.}

- **Physics:** Awarded to a scientist who demonstrated that beer froth obeys the mathematical law of exponential decay and decays exponentially with time.

- **Interdisciplinary Research:** Awarded to a scientist who performed a comprehensive survey of belly button lint, which concluded that you are most likely to have belly button lint if you are male, older, have an innie, and are somewhat hairy. *{This includes overall body hairiness and also presence of a snail trail (also called a happy trail), the line of hair leading from the pubic hair to the belly button. Some folks (they gotta be dudes) also call it a "treasure trail."}*

- **Chemistry:** Awarded to a scientist who made a conference table with a periodic table tabletop, with each grouping of elements made from a different wood.

- **Math:** Awarded to a team that made an analytical report estimating the total surface area of an Indian elephant (spoiler: 17.18 square meters).

- **Literature:** Awarded to a team that reported on the effects of prior bad textbook highlighting on reading comprehension, concluding that it negatively affects comprehension and accuracy.

- **Hygiene:** Awarded to the inventor of a washing machine for cats and dogs called Lavakan. *{It doesn't have a spin cycle, if you're wondering.}*

- **Economics:** Awarded, with snark, to Enron and other company contributors to the recession for "adapting the mathematical concept of imaginary numbers for use in the business world."

The 2002 award show, held at Harvard University, also featured the Win-a-Date-with-a-Nobel-Laureate Contest, though I suspect most Nobel Laureates don't make for a good date.

Venture over to Ig Nobel's website and read about the other winners. I'll see you back here in a year or three.

He Was a Busy Man

A friend's daughter is taking a food science course. That's what school should be all about, if you ask me. Teach science through food, and then maybe it would stick.

The daughter mentioned that Borden's milk is named for a guy named Borden (imagine that!) who invented condensed milk, which allowed milk to be transported.

I looked up Gail Borden Jr. and found this list of jobs he had along the way:

> County surveyor in Mississippi
> School teacher in Mississippi
> Surveyor in Texas, where he plotted the towns of Houston and Galveston and helped create the state's first topographical map
> Publisher of the first newspaper in Texas
> Delegate to the Convention of 1833, where he helped write early drafts of the Republic of Texas Constitution
> Republic of Texas collector of customs
> Secretary and agent at the Galveston City Company, where he helped sell 2,500 lots of land for $1.5 million
> Experimenter in disease cures and mechanics
> Developer of a terraqueous machine, a sail-powered wagon that would travel over land and sea

Developer of a dehydrated meat product, which he
    called the "meat biscuit"
Developer of condensed milk, which was long-lasting
    and required no refrigeration
Developer of juice from condensed fruits, including
    apples and grapes

Good grief. I was a teller and then a lawyer, and that
wore me the hell out.

What Is Tempeh, Anyway?

My daughter Mackenzie is in town from DC, where she is
going to college. Okay, okay, I'll get off the couch and go to
lunch with her. The sacrifices we make for our children.

My first dining outing, and I'm already confused. Just
when I learn how to pronounce quinoa and to tell the difference between quinoa and farro, they bring in the tempeh
tacos. WTF is that? Isn't tempeh just a different type of tofu?
If so, it would help my southern-fried brain if they'd just call
it "little balls of tofu."

Both tempeh and tofu are soy, it seems. Tempeh is made
from whole, soaked soybeans, while tofu is made from soy
pulp. Tempeh has an earthy, nutty flavor. Tofu, on the other
hand, doesn't have much flavor, instead taking on the flavor
of the seasoning. {So they say. In my experience, tofu always
tastes pretty much like eraser, no matter what they bathe it in.}

Okay, I'll order the tempeh tacos, but only because soy is
rumored to control hot flashes.

Sour Gum

While we were at lunch, Mackenzie said, "What is sorghum?"

"What brought that up?" I said.

"I don't know. I just thought about it."

"A commodity?" I was guessing.

"What kind of commodity?"

"I don't know. Wheat or something? Some kind of grainy farm product, I think."

"Do you cook with it?"

"Oh no, I never cook," I said.

But her question deserves more than a sassy answer. What exactly is sorghum? Seriously, what is it?

It's a grain. In the United States, sorghum is primarily used for animal feed and to make ethanol. Ethanol, in turn, is used to make beauty products, solvents, cleaning products, food extracts, and fuel. Solvent and fuel and food. Yum.

Sorghum has always been popular for human consumption in other parts of the world, particularly in Africa and Asia. In their raw form, sorghums look like pale pellets, similar to kernels of corn or small white beans. *{The plural really is sorghums. It looks weird, doesn't it? The whole word is weird, if you look at it long enough: sorg-hums.}*

To cook the sorghums, you simply boil them, like you would rice.

Sorghum consumption is now on the rise in the United States. Why? For one, it's gluten free. It's also full of protein. And as chef-driven restaurants are looking more toward the ancient grains, sorghum is finding itself on fancy menus.

So move on over, tempeh. You're dead to me.

Parmigiano-Reggiano

During my TV watching (was it *Top Chef*, maybe? *Bachelorette*? *Big Brother*? God, this list is getting embarrassing), I heard that Parmigiano-Reggiano cheese is not vegetarian. I'm curious why that would be.

Now I know. But first, a warning. Sometimes it's best not to know how your food is made. If this is one of those times

All the Food and Drink

for you, turn the page. If you want to keep reading, don't say I didn't warn you.

This is how Parmigiano-Reggiano is made. The cow is milked in the evening. The milk is put in a vat, where the cream separates and is skimmed. The skimmed milk is mixed with the cow's morning milk and warmed. And here's the nonvegetarian part: they add rennet so the milk will curdle. Then they cook the mixture, squeeze the water out, cook more, put the cheese in a salt bath, and age it for at least twelve years.

What is rennet? Enzymes from the fourth stomach chamber of an unweaned calf. How do they get the rennet from the stomach chamber? At slaughter.

Man, oh man, does that suck, because I love Parmigiano-Reggiano. Of course, I eat other slaughtered animals, so why is this one particularly bothersome? Because it's a calf. A baby.

Damn, I wish I hadn't looked this one up.

There is a difference between Parmigiano-Reggiano and Parmesan cheese, by the way, though rennet is used in making both. Parmigiano-Reggiano is a DOP product, so no other product is exactly like it. Parmesan is just a cheap imitation.

What's a DOP product? It is a product that has met the standards of and earned Italy's Denominazione di Origine Protetta label (Protected Designation of Origin), which provides a guarantee that the product and its ingredients are made in the area of origin, using traditional ingredients and methods.

The less strict Indicazione Geografica Protetta certification (Indication of Geographic Protection, or IGP) guarantees that at least one (but not necessarily all) of the phases of production come from the area of origin.

Other foods with DOP designations (if labeled) include the following:

- Mozzarella di bufala (from Campania or Lazio), made from water buffalo milk. Some cheeses called *mozzarella di bufala* do not have the DOP label and are made from cow's milk. These cow's milk cheeses, which should properly be called *fior di latte*, are less creamy than true *mozzarella di bufala*. {*Mozzarella di bufala is packaged in what looks like water but is actually whey; it helps keep the cheese moist so should not be discarded.*}
- Balsamic vinegar (from Modena and Reggio Emilia), which is more thick, rich, and aged than other vinegars.
- San Marzano tomatoes (from Campania), which are considered to have a more balanced flavor than other tomatoes.
- Olive oil (various regions).

Wines have a separate labeling structure, with these certifications (from least to most stringent):

- DO (Denominazione di Origine, or Designation of Origin)
- IGT (Indicazione Geografica Tipica, or Indication of Geographical Typicality)
- DOC (Denominazione di Origine Controllata, or Controlled Designation of Origin)
- DOCG (Denominazione di Origine Controllata e Garantita, or Controlled and Guaranteed Designation of Origin)

This system is like our "Look for the Union Label" but much better tasting.

Just Don't Bee

Reading about vegetarian stuff makes me wonder about vegans. What all can they not eat?

For one, honey.

How did I not realize vegans don't eat honey? It makes sense, given that vegans don't eat animals or their byproducts. But do you know what doesn't make sense? In my little pea brain, I wasn't thinking of insects as animals. It's not like I thought of them as plants or fungi, but I somehow categorized insects separately. Basically, I substituted "mammals" for "animals" in my own made-up taxonomy.

There's a ton of other stuff vegans can't eat:

- Cochineal or carmine, which is made by crushing the cochineal insect and is used for red food coloring in sodas, candy, or other "red" foods like Betty Crocker red velvet cake mix.
- Gelatin, which is made from the skin, bones, and connective tissue of cows and pigs.
- Isinglass, which is made from fish bladders and often used in wine and beer.
- Castoreum, which is made from secretions from a beaver's anal scent gland and most often used to calm anxiety. {*How did this discovery happen? "Oh gosh, I'm so keyed up these days. I think I may just go find a beaver and express its anal glands to see if that soothes me a bit."*}
- Omega 3 fatty acids, if made from fish. Plant-based omega 3s (seaweed, walnuts, edamame, kidney beans, and chia, hemp, and flax seeds) are vegan-friendly.
- Shellac. First, let me say I'm shocked that anyone eats shellac, but apparently it is sometimes used as a candy

glaze or coating on produce. I'm also surprised to learn shellac is made from the female lac insect. {*What did I think shellac was made from? I don't know, maybe gasoline or plastic?*}

- Vitamin D3, if made from fish oil or the lanolin in sheep wool. Plant-based vitamin D3 (e.g., lichen) is vegan-friendly.
- Dairy ingredients, including whey, casein, and lactose.

Other foods vegans have to be careful about, because they often contain animal products, include bean products (might contain lard or ham), beer and wine (might contain egg white albumin, gelatin, casein, or isinglass), bread products (might contain L-cysteine, made from poultry feathers), Caesar dressing (might contain anchovy paste), candy (might contain gelatin, carmine, shellac), dark chocolate (might contain dairy), french fries (might contain animal fat), fried foods (might contain eggs), non-dairy creamer (might contain casein, a protein derived from milk), tapenade (might contain anchovies), pesto (might contain parmesan), potato chips (might contain dairy), produce (might contain beeswax or shellac coatings), refined sugar (might contain bone char), roasted peanuts (might contain gelatin), and Worcestershire sauce (might contain anchovies).

What foods are safe for vegans? Fruits and vegetables, legumes, nuts and seeds, bread, rice and pasta, and dairy alternatives (provided they don't include any of the animal products listed above).

That's a lot of allowed foods, I suppose. But there's no way I'm going on a diet where you have to be suspect of dark chocolate and wine and you can't eat bacon.

Punt It

Rob and I went out to dinner (I'm venturing out, folks!). As we sat and drank our wine, I asked why there was a dent in the bottle.

"A dent? Show me," Rob said.

"This big one at the bottom," I said.

"The punt?"

"I call it a dent."

"But it's called a punt."

"Okay, but whatever it's called, why?"

Rob didn't know, but he was curious too.

Wine bottles were originally made by glassblowers. The glassblowers attached a rod (called a pontil rod) to the base of the bottle, to hold it while they formed it. When the bottle was completed, they snapped off the rod. To avoid leaving a scar with a sharp point that prevented the bottle from standing level, the glassblower used the rod to push a dimple into the bottom. That indentation is called a punt or kick-up. Now that bottles are made by machines and have no scars, punts are mostly unnecessary.

Some people say the punt still has some good uses though:

- It helps collect sediment in the wine.
- It makes the bottle appear to have more wine than it does.
- It helps distribute pressure within the bottle.
- It allows bottles to stack with the neck of one resting in the punt of another.
- It allows for easier pouring by leaving a place for the thumb.

Do I care about the punt one way or another, provided the wine is good? Nope. I'd drink it out of a nonpunted shampoo bottle if it was good enough. Well, probably not shampoo, but conditioner definitely.

We're Watching You Eat

Mackenzie and I are going to lunch again. Like most days, Mackenzie wants Whataburger. If you don't know about Whataburger, it's a Texas-based hamburger chain that sells the best darn burgers in the world, or so its devout fan base says. I'm not into Whataburger (which may put my Texas heritage into question), leaving us with Mackenzie's second choice: Tex-Mex.

We decide on Pete's Takos, because every San Antonian loves Pete's. We punch it into Google Maps, and it tells us the place is busy.

How does Google know? Is this real-time data, historical, or voodoo magic? I know Google is always spying on us, but do they know where we're eating?

Yup, they do. To develop visit data, Google uses aggregated data from actual visits within the past few weeks by people who have opted into Google location history. This data includes popular visit times, live visit information, wait times, and typical visit duration.

Wow. Google knows everything.

I wonder if its mind is ever blown by how popular a place is. Does it think, "Seriously? Why the heck is everyone here? It's just another taco place." But Google, you're missing critical context. They're not just any tacos. They're Pete's tacos.

Moooooo

Mackenzie told me milk doesn't need to be refrigerated. Wait, what?

Turns out she's both right and wrong.

In the United States, most milk is pasteurized. Pasteurization heats the milk, killing most of the harmful bacteria. But because the process doesn't kill all of the bacteria, the milk has a short shelf life and must be refrigerated.

Milk can also be subject to ultra-high pasteurization, where it is heated to high hell, killing all of the bacteria. This milk doesn't need to be refrigerated when put in aseptic, or sterile, packaging and unopened (like Mini Moos).

This reminds me of one of my favorite stupid jokes:

Knock knock.

Who's there?

Interrupting cow.

Interrupting cow wh—

Moooo.

It's a little hard to type, but the idea is that while the person is saying, "Interrupting cow who?" you interrupt them—like an interrupting cow would do.

Best. Joke. Ever.

For those of us with low standards, of course.

Proof It

Rob and I went out for drinks. Are you noticing that most of my paragraphs are starting with "[Person] and I went out for [food or drink]"? This project is working just as I hoped it would. Knowing that I have an assignment is making it easier for me to venture out in the world. There's only so much food and drink knowledge I can pick up in the house, so my assignment forces me to the streets.

Today's boozy curiosity: What does alcohol proof mean?

Proof is double the percentage of alcohol by volume. So if the alcohol is 20 percent alcohol by volume (ABV), it's 40 proof. Everclear, which may just kill you, is 190 proof, meaning it's 95 percent alcohol.

The term "proof" came about in England in the 1500s, when spirits were taxed based on how much alcohol they contained. If a liquid could ignite (generally at 50 percent ABV), there was proof of alcohol, and the liquid would be taxed.

The concept of proof isn't used with anything below 40 proof, which is why you never hear about the proof of wine or beer (with the average wine ranging from 11 to 13 percent and most beers ranging from 4 to 7 percent ABV).

Oh good. I didn't want to have to set my beer on fire.

We're Watching You Drink
Remember when I said I was going to show restraint while doing this part of Project Couch to Curiosity? That I was going to be careful not to do too much drinking? Well, oops, I did it again. Rob and I went out for drinks again.

It's probably time to consider reining it in, but in the interim, guess what I was curious about? Why bars have mirrors behind the bottles.

There is no definitive answer, but there are all sorts of theories:

- So the bartender can keep an eye on patrons, both to give them good service and to make sure they're not about to bonk him on the head and steal his cash drawer.
- So patrons (especially the ones back in the Wild West) can make sure they're not about to be bonked on the head.
- So the bar looks bigger.
- So the bar looks better stocked.
- So patrons can check each other out without having to be so obvious about it.

Is that also why some dudes have mirrors behind their beds? So they look bigger and better stocked?

Hands of Ham

Whenever I come across something I need to learn about, I write it down. I have about a thirty-second window to add the question to the list I keep on my phone. Any longer and the curiosity flits away, never to be recalled.

You will understand my urgency, then, when Rob and I were doing laundry last night and I came across something I was curious about. I linebackered through Rob to get to my phone. *{Or maybe I running backed. I should know more about the game if I'm going to make football analogies.}*

"What are you doing?" Rob said.

"I have to write something down on the learning list, quick, before I forget," I said.

"What?"

"Tide Pods."

"Aren't you learning about food and booze?"

"Yeah. But you know with the Tide Pod challenge, kids were eating the pods. And I wonder how that started. So I put it on the list."

"Aren't you getting a little ham-handed?" Rob said.

"Meaning?"

"It's a stretch. Like you're forcing things into the topic."

"Ham-handed! Ham's a food! I'm writing that down."

Rob shrugged his shoulders.

He's probably right. It probably is a stretch to fit Tide Pod learning into food month. But learning about hams? That's legit.

So what's the real reference with the phrase ham-handed? Your hands are big enough to hold hams? Your hands are as heavy as hams? Your hands look like big hams?

First, the definition: clumsy, heavy-handed.

The internet has various explanations for the origin of the phrase, but the one that makes the most sense to me goes like this:

Ham: Means unskillful, showy performer

Ham-fisted: Refers to an unskilled, showy pugilist (boxer)

Then ham-fisted morphed to ham-handed along the way.

This phrase has absolutely nothing to do with bacon, even though most things in life circle back to bacon—a good life, anyway.

Cuts of Beef

Rob and I had dinner out again, for Restaurant Week. {If you're curious (I was!), Restaurant Week was started in 1992 in New York City by Tim Zagat (of the Zagat Surveys) and Joe Baum (a restauranteur who originally created Windows on the World at the World Trade Center). The week was timed to coincide with the 1992 Democratic National Convention. It was so successful that it was continued in later years, expanded to a one-month event, and replicated in cities across the globe.}

You see, friends? I'm a gal about town now! I knew food and drink could draw me out. If there's one thing that can lure me, it's a calorie.

"I always order the filet, but they have tenderloin too," I said to Rob.

"Okay," he said.

"But I don't know the difference really, between filet and tenderloin."

"Really?"

"Oh, you do?" I said. "Explain it to me."

"Um, tenderloins are bigger."

"That's it? That's all you know?"

"Okay, you caught me. I don't know either," he said. "I'll ask the waiter."

"No, I'll ask."

When the waiter came up, this is what I said: "I'd like the ratatouille, please."

Rob rolled his eyes, because he knows how I am. I don't like bothering waiters with questions. I never complain about my food, no matter how wrong it is. They could bring me beef Stroganoff when I ordered asparagus, and I'd say, "Oh, no, it's fine. I've been kind of craving beef Stroganoff all week anyway." He can't understand how I can be an assertive woman in every other area of my life but completely submissive when I cross the threshold of any eating establishment. "Because they have spit in the kitchen, duh," I say. "Besides, I feel bad that they have to deal with asshole patrons all day."

Since Rob was no use to me in figuring out the difference between a filet and a tenderloin, and since I was no use to me either, I figured I should look it up.

To start, here's the cow:

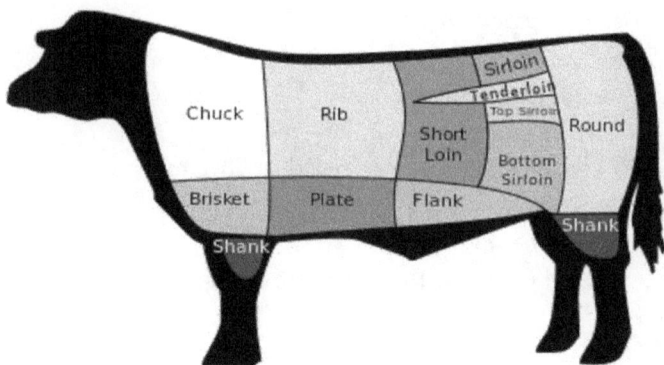

The closer the meat is to the legs or the shoulders, the tougher it is, because that is where all the muscle work is done.

- **Tenderloin.** This is a large, long muscle toward the back of the cow that does very little work, so the meat is tender.
- **Filet mignon.** Filet refers to the way the meat is cut, not a type of steak. Filet just means a cut of meat without bones. If it's a filet mignon (translation: a cute little filet), then it is a specific piece of meat—the little pointy end of the tenderloin (the part that cuts into the short loin). The filet mignon is a small, boneless, tender piece of meat, and my fave.
- **Chateaubriand.** This steak comes from the wider portion of the tenderloin. The chateaubriand is big and thick and thus harder to cook. Cook it too little, and you have a bloody slaughter on the plate. Cook it too much, and it's like a big old piece of beef jerky. I'd stick to the filet mignon. It's less fickle. *{The steak was named after François-René de Chateaubriand in the 1800s when the aristocrat was the French ambassador to England. His personal chef prepared the meat by roasting it between two lesser cuts of meat, which enhanced the steak's flavor and juiciness.}*
- **New York strip.** The strip is cut from the short loin. It's still tender but not quite as tender as the tenderloin/filet mignon.
- **T-bone and porterhouse**. The T-bone and porterhouse are both cuts from the short loin, where the tenderloin juts in. They both have tenderloin/filet mignon on one side of the T-shaped bone and a New York strip on the other. The porterhouse is cut closer to the rear end of the short loin, so it has more of the tenderloin on it than the T-bone.
- **Standing rib roast.** That's like a rack of lamb, except it's beef. It comes from the rib section, which is actually ally ribs six through twelve of the cow.

- **Prime rib.** This is the same meat as the standing rib roast, except it's deboned. Yeah, I know I said earlier that the preferred word is "boned" instead of "deboned," but I think that only applies to chicken and fish. Who knows if that's true, but I like "deboned" better, so that's what I'm using.
- **Ribeye.** The ribeye comes from the same place as prime rib and is the steak cut between one rib and the next. A ribeye isn't as tender as a filet mignon, but some people find it tastier because it's fattier.
- **Sirloin.** Sirloin comes from the back of the cow, where there is more muscle, so it's chewy. I don't like my beef chewy—or my chicken or fish or toothpaste either—so I'll skip the sirloin.
- **Flank.** The flank runs along the stomach and has a lot of fibers in it. You'll want to marinate it and cut it in strips against the grain, like for fajitas. *{A local restaurant advertised its sizzling fajitas. My oldest son, Thomas, liked to pronounce it "sizzling fa-jī-tus" so the dish sounded like a vaginal problem. He also pronounced local restaurant Vegeria as "vu-gee-ree-uh," and now I can't eat there anymore.}*
- **Brisket.** It's yum.

And the rest of the shit you just won't eat, so I'm done.

What Are Those Sneakers About?

The beef thing made me curious about sneakers. What's the segue, you ask? What do sneakers have to do with beef? Absolutely nothing, but it's a good example of how my brain hops from here to there, making connections along the way. There is always some logical progression to the thoughts.

I told you that the steak question came up from Restaurant Week. While I was writing the steak part, I decided to focus on just a few of the steaks, because I thought writing about every cut of meat wouldn't be fun.

Where does the word "fun" come from, anyway? I had to look that up. From Middle English "fonne," meaning a foolish person.

And here's where the sneakers leap comes in. I thought of fun, and then thought of how much fun I'd had with Mackenzie the day before. She and I had been driving near our house when I noticed a cross in an electrical wire.

"What do you think that is? A city electrical guy pushing religion on us?" I said.

"I think it's probably an electrical connection," Mackenzie said.

What she said next is why I love having Mackenzie in town.

"We should walk over to the police station to see if they know."

"Yes, that's exactly what we should do," I said, because for every overzealous cop you distract with questions about electrical wires, you save one person from an unnecessary pat-down.

We found a cop and asked him.

The cop didn't know either, but here's what he said: "Wouldn't it be weird if it were some sort of religious memorial?"

A cop who thinks like I do and uses the subjunctive. Astounding.

As Mackenzie and I walked home, we started talking about shoes on electrical lines. She thought they were a "drugs sold here" sign. I thought they were a "kid died here" sign. Turns out, they signal either a place where a gang murder happened or a place to buy drugs. Cool, Mackenzie and I were both right!

But do you know what my research says is the main reason for hanging sneakers? Are you ready for this? *Fun.* Full circle.

Want a Toque?

A Canadian friend posted this on Facebook: "There's lots of Canadian know-how you take for granted, such as where to store your mitts, scarf, and toque when you arrive indoors."

I could use me some of that know-how. Where do you store them? In the entryway? On a peg? In the oven? But all of those questions are second to this one: What is a toque?

Turns out it's Canadian for a knit cap—like the pompom kind Ralphie wore in *A Christmas Story*—and pronounced "tuque."

But guess what else a toque is? A chef's hat—pronounced "toke"—like the cute little one Remy wore in *Ratatouille.*

And you know what you can put in ratatouille? Bacon. Again, it all comes back to bacon.

Life's Short, Desert First

I had yet another "How the hell did I not know that?" moment.

It turns out that the phrase "getting your just desserts"—meaning something like "You've got it coming to you, biatch!"—is actually "getting your just deserts," with one *s* (though it's pronounced like the confection dessert, not like the Sahara Desert).

That makes no sense. It's like saying "Karma is coming for you, and it's going to send you to an arid region." Turns out the phrase comes from an older definition of the word "desert," which meant a reward or punishment you deserved.

Well, there's some good learning. It's also a good time to remember that desert the verb (as in, to leave) and desert the noun (as in, arid plain) are homographs—words spelled the same but with different meanings. More specifically, they're a subtype of homographs called heteronyms—words that are spelled the same, have different meanings, and are pronounced differently.

You can probably come up with other heteronyms, if you deliberate in a deliberate way. Don't attribute the attributes of a heteronym to any old word though. You'll have to moderate yourself and be moderate about which words you call heteronyms. You'll need to separate heteronyms from separate types of words—like homonyms, say.

Now you're wondering about homonyms, aren't you? Well, head on over to the "Sherpa, Sherpa" section in the chapter "All the Words." We'll wait.

Waiting.

Waiting.

Waiting.

You're back! I hope you were content with its contents.

A Restaurant, I Think

I suggested to Rob that we go out to dinner. We've always been go-out-to-dinner types, but typically we've done that on weekends. Now we have an excuse to go out every night of the week.

"Again?" Rob said.

"I wish there were another option, but y'know, Project Couch to Curiosity."

So off Rob and I went, to dinner at a local restaurant called Tre Trattoria.

"What is a trattoria anyway?" I asked Rob.

"A restaurant, I think," he said.

"Then what's a ristorante?"

"A restaurant, I think."

"Is there any question I can ask that you won't give that answer to?"

"A restaurant, I think," he said.

Sometimes Rob is so clever.

But really, what's a trattoria? And how is a trattoria different from an enoteca or an osteria or a ristorante?

From most fancy to least fancy:

- Ristorante: A fine dining, chef restaurant.
- Trattoria: A family-friendly restaurant with typical Italian food and usually a chalkboard menu.
- Osteria: Historically, a wine bar with simple local food or bring-your-own picnic food. It has evolved to be extra casual dining, with a regional focus and often with communal tables.
- Enoteca: A wine tasting bar with limited (if any) food.
- Taverna: A wine pub with simple food.

Italy also has regular bars, some of which may serve an *aperitivo*, a predinner drink accompanied by light food (similar to the American happy hour, but good). Some also offer *apericena*, which is the same concept but with heavier food that could serve as dinner.

I'm mostly a trattoria or osteria type. I love chef-fy food but only in a casual vibe. White tablecloths make me uncomfortable. And I like good service but not overly good service. I hate it when I take one sip of wine, and as soon as I put the glass down the waiter is leaning over me to refill my glass, breathe on my neck, or maybe cop a feel.

In fact, I hate the whole pomp around wine. I don't like tasting the first pour. I hate that while I take the first sip, the waiter has to stand there cradling the bottle with the label facing me. I hate how the waiter sets down the cork just so. I wish they'd just toss the bottle on the table and let me chug it from there.

Anyhow, go to Tre Trattoria when you get the chance.

It's a restaurant, I think.

!?
All the Exercise

Putting a spotlight on food and drink makes me want more of both, and I already want them plenty so I figure it's time I move on.

This month I've decided to focus on . . . oh shoot, I don't even want to say it, because then it'll be some sort of commitment, a commitment I know I won't keep. Okay, okay, here goes . . . exercise.

Retirement has been a letdown on the exercise front. I should have known that if exercise wasn't a priority before retirement, it wouldn't be after. But I tricked myself into thinking I wasn't exercising because I was working. In reality, I wasn't exercising because I wasn't exercising.

I have made exercise declarations since I quit work:

I'll do CrossFit!

Triathlon, that's what I'll do!

Swimming! I love to swim!

I'll take a daily walk instead!

Okay, forget daily. How about just three times a week?

Maybe I could just get up off the couch once or twice a week?

In truth, I never exercise unless all three of these criteria are met:

1. My husband invites me for a walk.
2. It's not raining. Nor is it too hot. Not too dark either. Nor too cold. And absolutely no wind.
3. I have nothing I can say I am busy with.

Under those three circumstances, and only those three circumstances, will I move my body in any way that would help it survive.

For this phase of Project Couch to Curiosity, I'll have to move my ass, so I can learn and write about ass-moving.

I talked to my youngest son, Clark, about my plan. I interrupted his first-person shooter game to have the conversation, so our discussion was necessarily brief.

"Just checking in on you, Sweetie," I said.

"Okay."

"What's up with you?"

"Nothing."

"Any exciting plans for the day?"

"No."

"Well, my day is looking pretty good. I am going to start exercising today! I decided to focus on exercise all month. I'm hoping that will make me do it. What do you think of my plan?"

"Okay," he said.

"Any tips for me?"

"No."

"Nothing, really?"

"Ummmm. Write about other people exercising—maybe sports—'cuz you're not gonna do it," he said.

God, this kid knows me.

Okay, okay. I'll modify. For this phase, I will either write about me moving my ass or others moving theirs. That's far more realistic. Of course, I'll have to do my laundry, taxes, crossword puzzle, travel planning, meditation, thank you notes, stretching, window washing, list making, online shopping, and annual pap smear before I can even think about starting to exercise.

Just Keep Swimming

You'll need some history of my exercise experience to understand how I got myself so firmly planted on the couch.

I had weight loss surgery many years ago. Weight loss surgeries, to be more accurate. First I got a Lap-Band, where the surgeon put an adjustable band around my stomach, like a small ring or inner tube. After the band was surgically placed (laparoscopically), it was filled with saline through a port implanted near my sternum. This caused the band to tighten around my stomach, like a tight belt, restricting how much my stomach could hold and thus how much I could eat.

The theory of the Lap-Band was good, but the reality was not. No matter how much saline was put in the band or removed from it, I would have so much restriction that I had a hard time eating anything but mush. A diet of creamy soups, mashed potatoes, and protein shakes may help you lose weight initially, but it's hardly sustainable.

After a few years of fighting with the Lap-Band, I had it removed (also laparoscopically). I gained weight—lots and lots of weight—and I felt like an absolute failure. Who ends up weighing more after weight loss surgery than before? Me, that's who.

As my weight increased to dangerous levels, my doctor persuaded me that I needed to try again. I had a gastric bypass. This surgery creates a small stomach pouch routed directly to the small intestine, bypassing most of the stomach and the first part of the small intestine. The surgery restricts both how much you can eat and how much the body will absorb. And this surgery? Successful, you'll be glad to know. Fucking finally.

Anyhow, before the gastric bypass, exercise was really out of the question. Mostly, the embarrassment. When you're extremely overweight, your body sloshes about, and there's really no containing it. Folks may deny having bad thoughts about obese people exercising, saying things like, "It's just good they're out there." But when you exercise, those same folks stare at you, and you know they're thinking, "Good grief. Show some self-control, lady!"

Once I was at a public swimming pool—which was quite brave of me because bathing suit—and a young child looked at me and asked, "Why are you so faaaaat?"

"Why are you such a little asshole?" I said.

Okay, I didn't, but I definitely wanted to. Instead I choked out something like, "Well, people are just different."

Besides the embarrassment, there are difficult logistics with exercise when you're extremely overweight. Imagine putting another person on your back, then trying to jog around the block. That extra person would be flopping about, and you'd have to stop every five feet to get her resituated. Also, you wouldn't be able to breathe after about ten feet. Your heart just couldn't hold the load. Some think obese people should just eat less and exercise, but the problem is that we can't really exercise. And then we're uncomfortable in our bodies and ashamed of ourselves, and we use food to cope. It's a sad cycle.

When I had weight loss surgery, I had a chance to break that cycle. My stomach was teaspoon-sized, so I lost weight, so I was able to begin exercise, so I was able to keep off the weight. It was a sort of control-alt-delete on my life. {If you were born in the Mac era, don't you think my crowd is a little too old for you? Just saying . . . Anyhow, back in the old days when there were no Macs, just PCs, control-alt-delete was the way you cleared and restarted your computer after you mucked it up. And if you didn't try this before bothering the office IT guy for help, he shivved you. And if you did try rebooting before annoying the IT guy, he shivved you anyway.}

Even heavy, I could swim, since swimming is a weight-neutral sport. But after I lost some weight, I wanted to give bike riding a try. I hoped it was true that riding a bike is a skill you don't forget even after twenty-five years. One day I walked into a bike shop and asked them to fix me up.

"What kind of bike are you looking for?" the salesperson asked.

"A girl bike."

I hadn't ridden a bike since my only choice was a banana seat with a basket and a bell, daisy stickers optional.

I left the bike shop with a hybrid bike, a cross between a mountain bike and a road bike—a general all-purpose bike that would work nicely on the hike-and-bike trails we had near the house. When I first got on the bike, I did remember how to ride, and cycling made me feel freeeeeeeee.

Soon after that, and about three years after I got divorced from my first husband, I started dating a guy. I mentioned I was toying with the idea of trying out triathlon. "You know, now that I'm swimming and cycling. I'd just have to learn to run."

"Um, I don't think so," he said.

"Why are you such a little asshole?" I said.

Okay, I didn't say it that time either, but I absolutely should have. That he was an asshole was all the push I needed.

I signed right up for a triathlon training group and ended things with the guy.

I felt athletic for the first time in my life. I was one of those "picked last" kids, but school tested you on speed and agility, which were skills my body would never be good at. Triathlon taught me that even if you're slow, determination and endurance are good for something.

Over time I did longer and longer distance triathlons, until ultimately I shifted to Ironman, which is a 2.4-mile swim, 112-mile bike, capped off by a marathon. I know, it sounds insane. It is insane.

Ironman basically started as a dick-measuring contest. In 1977 after a race in Oahu, Hawaii, some runners were debating some swimmers about who was more fit. Someone suggested that cyclists might be the most fit of all. And a race, combining all three disciplines, was born. Whoever won would be crowned the Iron Man. The first race was held in Oahu in 1978. The first winner, Gordon Haller, was both a runner and a cyclist.

The race moved to Kailua-Kona in 1981. In 1982 the race got national attention when college student Julie Moss collapsed as she was about to cross the finish line in first place. She crawled to the finish line and came in second. The footage was widely broadcast, bringing attention to the sport.

The Kona race continues to this day, and it is now the world championship for the event. Other Ironman events are held throughout the globe, with thirteen Ironman races (give or take depending on the year) taking place in the United States annually.

Of course, I wouldn't have thought I could ever finish a full Ironman back when I was so overweight. But I worked my way up, from short sprint triathlons (750m swim, 20k bike,

5k run) to middle-distance Olympic triathlons (1.5k swim, 40k bike, 10k run), to longer-distance half Ironman events (1.2-mile swim, 56-mile bike, 13.1-mile run), and finally, after a full year of training up to twenty hours a week, to long-distance Ironman events (2.4-mile swim, 112-mile bike, 26.2-mile run).

In Ironman I could hold my own against twenty-somethings with their tight little agile bodies. They'd sprint off the start line, and as I lumbered mile by mile, I'd see them sprinkled on the side of the road. I finished far at the back of the pack, but I finished.

The bad part of Ironman, though, is that the training is like having a second job (and a third and a fourth). After my second Ironman event in 2015, I quit and have been safely planted on the sofa ever since. From 140.6 miles to couch.

So for my first effort at getting back to exercise, I decided to join a swim program. Maybe having a standing appointment for exercise would help.

Today was the first practice, and it kicked my ass. The class was full of those same twenty-something triathlete types with their tight little agile bodies, and then there was fifty-something me with her three-baby belly. It did feel good, though, trying to hold my own.

I always feel better when I'm exercising regularly—strong and athletic. I like seeing my arms become muscular and feeling comfortable wearing short-sleeved tops again. I appreciate that I carry myself differently when I get out of the pool, with a broader shoulder and a confident step. I know exercising helps me stave off depression, if I can only keep it going.

When the newness of this wears off and I start finding excuses for skipping workouts, until all I am doing is watching *Downton Abbey* and not leaving the house, will you please remind me how good I felt about myself today? I'd appreciate it.

Solvitur Ambulando

I don't need to get all complicated about exercising. If I just walked, that would help. You may have heard the phrase *solvitur ambulando*—"It is solved by walking."

I've always thought that meant something like "Stop letting your brain spin out of control. Get up off the fucking couch and go for a walk, why don't cha? Give your brain some space to work things out."

But the phrase actually means a problem is solvable by demonstration. It comes from Greek philosopher Diogenes (the one who lived in a barrel in the marketplace and wandered around carrying a lantern during the day, saying he was looking for an honest man; he didn't find one). He responded to a claim that motion wasn't real by standing up and walking.

I like my definition better. It has curse words.

Louis Louis

I know I'm supposed to be doing exercise, but Clark said watching exercise counts, so today I'm watching tennis.

Rob likes tennis. Sometimes when he's watching, he'll say, "You've got to see this." If "this" means Serena, I'll be sucked in for the afternoon. Otherwise I'll watch the one replay he's excited about, then move about my day. Today is a Serena day.

Normally I'm not much of a tennis person, so I've not wondered out of the blue, until now, about the Louis Armstrong Stadium at Flushing Meadows, where they play the US Open. Why is it called the Louis Armstrong stadium? Was Louis Armstrong a tennis player?

No, he was not.

Louis Armstrong, the jazz musician, lived in Queens, New York, near Flushing Meadows. He died in July 1971. Tuck that in the back of your mind. I'll connect the dots in a bit—I promise.

The Newport Jazz Festival was held in Newport, Rhode Island, beginning in 1954.

In 1969 the festival added rock groups to the lineup (including Blood Sweat & Tears, the Jeff Beck Group, Jethro Tull, James Brown, and Led Zeppelin). The festival sold out, and folks unable to get tickets surged the fence to get in. In order to disperse the crowd, the festival announced that Led Zeppelin's set had been canceled. After the crowd thinned, Led Zeppelin was allowed to go on as scheduled.

In 1970 the festival reverted to an all-jazz lineup, and the event was—uneventful. But in 1971 the festival added rock group the Allman Brothers Band to the lineup. Again the event sold out, and stoned-out-of-their-brains kids unable to get into the show surged the fence. The drugged-up teens rushed the stage, destroying equipment and sending three hundred people to the hospital.

The city of Newport grew weary of the mayhem, so in 1972 the festival moved to New York.

To celebrate the arrival of the jazz festival in Flushing Meadows renamed its court after jazz great Armstrong, who lived nearby and had recently died.

See? I told you I'd connect the dots. I always do.

Yellow Balls
Speaking of tennis, I recently learned why tennis balls are yellow.

Initially players used white tennis balls. But when color TV came around, the white balls were hard to follow on television, since they matched the white lines of the court.

The International Tennis Federation did a study, which officially concluded that yellow tennis balls were easier to follow on color television. In 1972 they changed ITF rules to require that all tennis balls be white or yellow. Most tournaments immediately switched to yellow balls to accommodate color-television viewing. Interestingly, Wimbledon—being in England, a country steeped in tradition and slow to make changes (or so they say)—didn't switch to yellow balls until 1986.

You know what color ball would be even easier to follow on television? A rainbow-patterned, glow-in-the-dark tennis ball that leaves a trail of hot-pink glitter dust behind it as it soars through the air. But those fuddy-duddies at Wimbledon will probably never go for it. Rave haters.

Precious Dimples

Now that I'm paying particular attention to exercise and sport (though not actually doing either), I'm realizing how much I don't know. I wouldn't expect to know sports rules, strategy, or player names. But you'd think I'd know some basic things, like why golf balls have dimples. I know they make the ball travel farther, but why?

Here's what *Scientific American* says: "Dimples on a golf ball create a thin turbulent boundary layer of air that clings to the ball's surface. This allows the smoothly flowing air to follow the ball's surface a little farther around the back side of the ball, thereby decreasing the size of the wake."

I understand each of the individual words in the paragraph, but I have no idea what they mean collectively. How do the dimples allow the air to follow the surface farther around the back side of the ball? Why does this matter? Who cares how big the wake is? What does all of this meeeeeean?

I searched for an explanation that made sense. I even watched videos with fancy graphics showing the pressure systems in front of and behind the ball and how those systems changed depending on the ball's dimpling. Like all things science, I can read the words, but somehow they don't translate into any sort of understanding.

What do I do in these situations? I text my daughter, Mackenzie, because she's way smarter than I am and has the patience to explain things to me.

> I'm trying to figure out why golf balls have dimples and my pea brain can't understand it. Something about turbulence and drag and lift and WTF? Can you figure it out and explain it to me like I'm a little dumb baby?

And sweet Mackenzie is so used to having a dumb baby for a mama that she obliged. She got me on a Zoom call, with a golf ball in hand for a visual aid, and taught me how things work.

When you strike the golf ball into the air, the ball displaces the air to move through it. As the ball goes through the air, it splits the air and the air wraps around each side of the ball. After the ball passes through, it leaves an air pocket behind it. This pocket is a low-pressure area—that is, an area where there is less air than there is elsewhere. Air pressure wants to equalize, and the low-pressure pocket will want to be filled. So the pocket will essentially grab at the ball and try to pull it back into the void, thus creating drag on the ball.

If the ball is smooth . . . {*I'm not saying I wondered this, but just in case you wondered, smooth is never spelled with an -e at the end. You're probably getting it confused with soothe. It's understandable.*}

If the ball is smooth, the air will whoosh off the ball in a straight line, leaving a large low-pressure pocket with air molecules organized in neat, hard-to-penetrate layers. If the ball has dimples, the air will move up and down over the ball as it passes over, staying closer to the ball and leaving a smaller low-pressure wake behind the ball. Moreover, the air molecules left behind the dimpled ball will be more chaotic and thus easier to fill than the organized layers left by the smooth ball. The smaller, more easily fillable void left by the dimpled ball will fill more quickly, reducing drag.

Here's a nice little picture that might help you visualize:

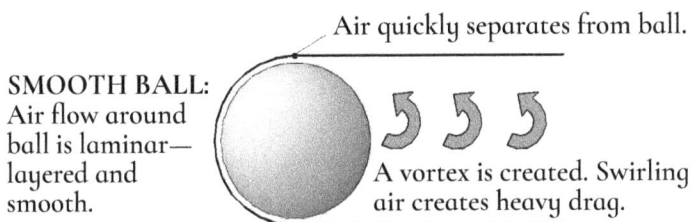

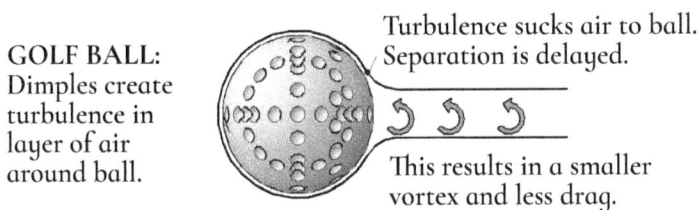

Air quickly separates from ball.

SMOOTH BALL:
Air flow around
ball is laminar—
layered and
smooth.

A vortex is created. Swirling
air creates heavy drag.

Turbulence sucks air to ball.
Separation is delayed.

GOLF BALL:
Dimples create
turbulence in
layer of air
around ball.

This results in a smaller
vortex and less drag.

Fore! Skin

In learning about golf ball dimples, I discovered that at one point golf balls were made of boiled goose feathers stuffed inside leather sacks, called featheries. These balls were expensive (because they were handmade), not durable, and unsuitable for wet conditions.

In 1848 the feathery was replaced with the gutta-percha ball, made from the rubbery sap of the sapodilla tree. In about 1900 the gutta-percha was replaced with the rubber ball, which was made of a solid core, wrapped with rubber thread, and covered with sap from the balata tree. It wasn't until the mid-1960s that the modern resin ball came to be.

And baseballs? Some reports say they were originally made of horse foreskins. And in the mid-1800s, they were made of a solid core wrapped in yarn or leather. What was this solid core made of? Often, a fish eye.

Footballs were originally made of animal bladders, stuffed with straw. And billiard balls were originally made from elephant tusk ivory. Soccer balls? Originally made of pig heads, before the use of them was deemed inhumane and they were replaced with balls made from inflated pig bladders. *{Apparently blowing up someone's bladder and making a kickball out of it is just the more caring thing to do.}*

What's the point here? Sports—they can be gross.

One of the problems with all of this new knowledge is that I feel the urge to share it. That sounds like a good share-the-wealth instinct, but the problem is I can't quite remember what I've learned. Here's how the conversations go:

"I'm so sorry for yawning, but I'm exhausted after my long run today," the skinny dude will say.

"A long run. That's impressive," I'll say.
"Oh, it was nothing. Just a 30k trail run. It only felt long because I had a beginner runner in front of me slowing me down."

"Did you know that footballs used to be made of penises?"
"Excuse me?"

"Or maybe it was bladders. Or both? It might have been baseballs, actually, and it might have been testicles."

"Ummm, okay?"

And I'll be fine with that conversation, because it got that trail-running jerk to back away from me, which was the goal. What I won't be fine with is that I've already forgotten one of the only things I've ever found interesting about sports. So I'll go home and relearn the learning.

Baseballs = horse foreskins

Footballs = animal bladders

Soccer balls = pig bladders

Then the next conversation will go like this:

"Did you know that baseballs used to be made of foreskins?" I'll say.

"Excuse me?"

"Not human foreskins, but animal. Maybe the pig? Except those would seem too little. Maybe pig foreskins could work for marbles, but they probably weren't the ones used for baseballs. Maybe it was dogs? But ewww. Hmmm. I can't quite remember."

And this is why Rob never stands next to me at parties.

My Parents' Obsessions

You know that swimming program I joined? It didn't stick. Already. Every day something has come up to keep me from going. What are these "somethings"? Last week they looked like this:

- Monday: Out of town
- Tuesday: Stomachache
- Wednesday: Doctor's appointment
- Thursday: Some interesting testimony on Capitol Hill I wanted to watch
- Friday: Who starts on a Friday?

All of these somethings are silly, of course. We all know that neither my stomachache nor my doctor's appointment lasted the entire day. When I was out of town, I could have come back earlier so I'd have time to exercise. And we certainly know that the Capitol Hill testimony was not all that riveting.

I need to find a way to get obsessed with exercise.

My parents are obsessives, so you'd think it would come more easily to me than to most. Here is a sampling of the obsessive phases they have gone through:

Mama	Daddy
Cello	Skeet shooting
Health food	Grilling steak
Liberal politics	Fox News
Photography	Movies
German literature in translation	Jesus
	Guns
Victrola records	CB radios
Classical music	Yahoo forums
Rare books	RV'ing
Mexican muralists	Sailing
Phoenix and Consolidated Glass	Scuba diving
	Gambling
Mission San José tiles	Twelve-step programs
Mexican postcard photography	
Animal Crossing	

After reading those lists, you probably gathered Mama and Daddy were not married for long.

The difference between me and my parents? They would work their interests until they became experts. *{Dad was a* *national skeet shooting champion. Mama has published books about tile and photography. These folks are serious about their expertise, trust me.}*

I work my interests until, yeah, whatever, time to move on. But I had a job and three kids; my folks both had self-employment and childcare providers. So I'd have time to half-ass do some things like playing bridge, horseback riding, and playing guitar, but when I didn't really have the talent or the time to be any good, well, on to something else.

So now, my curiosity: How do you make yourself want to exercise regularly? Specifically, what can I do to get myself to move again?

The internet tells me the secret to getting serious about something is to have a goal, then establish small, attainable steps to get you there. So that's what I'm going to try.

My ultimate goal: To exercise at least thirty minutes a day for five days. Attainable step for this week: Go for three days a week. Thirty minutes, three days. Easy-peasy.

I'll let you know how it goes, because the other secret? Accountability.

Low in Number

I'm curious about another sports thing. I should probably satisfy that curiosity before even thinking about doing any exercise, don't you think?

College basketball jerseys can't have the numbers six, seven, eight, or nine anywhere on them. Why is that?

Because when there is a foul, the official signals the offender by noting the first digit of the offender's jersey number with one hand and the second digit of the jersey number with the other. Most officials have only two hands, with five fingers on each hand. Five is the highest number that can be fingered, so it's the highest allowed in the ones or tens position of the jersey number. *{You know why we can be friends? Because you just tittered at the word "fingered."}*

What if the official is missing a finger? Do players have to change their numbers so four is the highest? I Googled it, but nothing. I guess it doesn't come up all that often.

Exercise in Accountability

Remember how I committed to exercise three times during the week and report back to you? Accountability effective! I exercised exactly three times last week—one swim, one bike, one run—and I'm reporting my success to you now. Goal fulfilled!

This week's goal: Same thing. Three exercise days and accountability. I know I should bump it up to four, but I'm not feeling it, so I'm going to make myself another attainable goal with the hope that meeting it will inspire me to continue.

Is this enough exercise to provide any meaningful health benefits? The Department of Health and Human Services recommends the following physical activity for adults each week:

- 150 to 300 minutes of moderate intensity, or 75 to 150 minutes of vigorous intensity
- At least two days of muscle strengthening activities of major muscle groups: legs, hips, back, chest, abdomen, shoulders, arms

So no, it's not enough. I need to add CrossFit two times a week. But I don't wanna, even though I'm paying for classes I'm not attending. That's how I roll. I join gyms and classes so I can feel better about myself, and then I don't go and end up feeling worse about myself because, well, don't we all do this? *{Yes, we do all do this. A 2019 article in the Hustle reported* *a study showing 63 percent of annual gym memberships are never used, 22 percent of members stop attending within six months of joining, and 82 percent of members attend less than once a week.}*

Anyhow, in a slight nod to "I really should be doing this," I will twice this week do some pushups—except I can't do pushups because my arms are too darn weak, so instead I'll do little stand-up pushes against the kitchen counter.

I'll report back to let you know how it went. Thanks for being my accountability coach (without even getting paid for it)!

Woulda, Shoulda, Coulda

I'm reporting back, like I said I would. I did not exercise, though I said I should. I will not exercise, though I know I could.

Black Eyes

This sport and exercise thing isn't panning out for me, so I'm skating through this learning focus by learning about other people's movement.

"Why do they wear black grease stuff under their eyes?" I asked Rob. He was watching a football game.

"It's called eye black," he said.

"But why?"

"It cuts the glare of the sun."

"But it's night."

"Oh, huh. You should research that."

The idea is that the eye blacks absorb light, cutting the glare of both the sun and stadium lights (thus useful day or night). The eye blacks also help wearers recognize contrast more easily (like incoming footballs or baseballs, say).

Do they work? Eye grease does have a minimal impact on glare, but the black stickers seem to have no effect.

Why do players wear the stickers if they have no effect? Because they look cool.

But cooler than the grease, which does work some? Apparently so.

Lesson: Don't question cool.

Down with Football

Speaking of football, you know that yellow line they show on TV to indicate how far the offensive players need to advance for a first down? It looks like the line is painted on the field, but you know it's not. How do they do that wizard magic?

At the beginning of the season, every football field is laser scanned, so the computer knows each field's particular contour and shades of grass. Before the game, the field's color palette is reviewed, as it will change depending on lighting and weather conditions. This information, along with information about the cameras being used for televising the game, is placed in a computer model, and a computer operator marks the ball placement and the first down line before each play.

The field acts as a green screen, so the line will be visible only where it would not be blocked by the players' bodies. The model knows to insert the line only on the shades of green of the field, not on any other colors that might be obscuring the field.

The technology works well but can have difficulty when uniform colors are similar to the grass color (for example, the Green Bay Packers in certain lighting) or when the color of the field changes during the game (say, in snow).

Do you know what this technology cannot do though? It cannot keep players from having head injuries. Until it does, no football watching for Lucie.

I know, I know, the NFL is devastated by my absence. Sometimes tough love is what it takes though.

Torture by Treadmill

If I'm not going to go out for a walk, maybe I should just walk on a treadmill. But damn, I hate treadmills.

Do you know why they are so awful?

Because they're instruments of torture. In the 1800s difficult prisoners were made to climb the "tread-wheel," a spoked paddle wheel. As the wheel turned, the spokes pumped water or crushed grain. A *Mental Floss* article quotes a former prison guard as saying it was the treadmill's "monotonous steadiness, and not its severity, which constitutes its terror."

That sums up my feelings perfectly.

My Bag of Tricks

You would think I'd have some sort of born inclination to sport. My father was in the Olympics, after all. Well, he was kind of in them. He was the national skeet shooting champion and a shoo-in for the 1968 Olympic team. Unfortunately he had an off day at the trials. He did not make the full team but was asked to join as an alternate. While Dad did join the team in Mexico City, he did not end up shooting, as none of the team members ended up getting injured or sick.

Every one of my friends knew about Dad's unfortunate luck—being the best but blowing the opportunity to show it. How did my friends know this? I told them, since this was a central story of my life, though it had nothing to do with me.

I talked to Dad about how disappointing it must have been to be on the Olympic team but not get to shoot.

"What? I wasn't on the Olympic team," Dad said.

"Well, an alternate, I mean," I said.

"I wasn't an alternate. I didn't even make it to the trials."

Wait, what?

All to say, I make up shit. I'm not intentionally a liar, but I weave these beautiful stories in my head and it seems I want you to share in them.

So a lesson for you for today: Don't trust a damn thing I say. I think I'm telling the truth, but sometimes I might be tricking you.

Speaking of tricks, what if I were to trick myself into wanting to exercise? I Googled it and found the best suggestion: Only wash your hair on days you work out. Your hair will get nasty, you will start to feel like bugs are climbing on your scalp, and eventually you'll go for a run just to make the itching stop. Yes, it sounds desperate, but maybe?

A Hat Trick

Still speaking of tricks, I know nothing about professional sports. Not only do I know nothing, I care nothing about them. Dallas Cowboys playing the Texas Rangers? One, I don't even know if that can happen, but I'm guessing it could. Two, why would I care who wins? It's just one business entity going up against another. Do I care if Apple beats out Samsung during a particular quarter? Nope, not a whit. What if Apple were to get cheerleaders? Would that change anything? Nope, nothing. A mascot? Sorry, no dice. I just don't care. That the business entity is a sports team does not ratchet up my emotional investment.

Given my general lack of interest in sports, it will be no surprise that I also have a general lack of knowledge about them.

All of which gets me to the question, What the heck is a hat trick?

The context: While watching a hockey game, Rob yelled out to me, "Hey babe. Check this out! Jakub just scored a hat trick! Look at the Nats' hats!"

"Very cool," I said, and went about my day.

Later I thought about it and realized I had no idea what he was talking about. Who is Jakub? What's a hat trick? What's with the hats?

In hockey, when a player scores three goals in a single game, they call it a hat trick (hatty for short, though I should point out that hatty has the same number of syllables as hat trick, so it's really not any shorter). The fans celebrate by throwing their hats onto the ice.

Jakub Vrána is a forward on the Washington Capitals hockey team. During a game against the Calgary Flames, he scored three goals, so the fans threw their hats on the ice.

Among the fans were players from the Washington Nationals baseball team, fresh off their World Series win. So when Vrána scored the hat trick, the Nats threw their World Series championship hats on the ice, which yes, is cool.

I also learned that while a hat trick is a good thing in hockey, it's a bad thing in baseball, where a hat trick is three strikeouts by the same player.

In football (or soccer, as we Americans call it), a hat trick is three goals in a game. In American football, the term isn't used, probably because scoring three touchdowns ain't no big thang.

So where does the term come from? Explanations abound, but the one that makes the most sense to me is that it comes from magicians pulling rabbits out of their hats. That shit's amazing.

And if you're now wondering how the rabbit hat trick works, I can help. Sometimes the magician has the rabbit

All the Exercise

77

up his sleeve and uses sleight of hand to pop the rabbit into the hat. But more often the hat has a hidden opening at the bottom. The magician puts the hat on a rabbit-containing chest, which also has a hidden opening. The magician reaches in and pulls the rabbit from the chest. Ta-da!

Twenty-Six Things

Obviously, the exercise portion of this project hasn't been very fruitful, and I fear only greasy-haired shame will motivate me. But I don't want to leave this chapter with shame. I'd like to get to exercise from a more positive frame of reference, so let me go back a bit.

In 2009, the night before my gastric bypass surgery, I made a list of what I hoped to gain from weight loss surgery. The list has twenty-six points on it. "That's an odd number," current me is thinking. "Why didn't prior me just chop one off and list twenty-five things? Or add four and list thirty?" Who knows. Maybe I was busy getting ready for surgery in the morning and didn't have time to add more. Maybe I knew I should chop it to twenty-five but couldn't pick a goal I wanted to give up. Or maybe I wasn't as nutso obsessive back then as I am now. Whatever my reasoning, here is the list:

1. To keep healthy so I can raise my children
2. To walk up a single flight of steps without gasping for air
3. To be able to take the stairs instead of the elevator
4. To be able to ride a bicycle
5. To be able to ride a horse
6. To be able to join my friends in their activities

7. To buckle the seatbelt in the car without effort
8. To be without foot pain
9. To be able to fit into shoes and boots
10. To be able to fit in chairs and booths
11. To stop being nervous about the vehicle tilting when I step into it
12. To be able to fit in airline seats
13. To not feel as if I am a nuisance to those around me or feel apologetic or embarrassed about having to sit next to someone I know I will bother
14. To be able to run
15. To be able to eat without feeling my tablemates are judging every bite of food I put in my mouth
16. To be able to wear a bathing suit in public
17. To avoid having people stare or make innocent but hurtful comments
18. To feel good about myself when I look in the mirror
19. To be able to meet or date someone
20. To avoid my children being embarrassed by my weight
21. To have more energy
22. To be able to buy clothes in regular department stores
23. To be relieved of the fear that I am growing out of the sizes that even the plus-size stores carry
24. To be able to dress in more stylish clothes and clothes more appropriate to the event I am attending

25. To stop surveying every room I enter to see if there might be other heavy people there
26. To be able to wash my feet, clip my toenails, and buckle or tie my shoes without effort

I love the goals I made. They weren't vain "I want to look hot" goals but "I want to be able to live, breathe, walk, climb, ride, sit, dress, eat, fly, run, swim" sorts of goals.

Some of these goals do make me sad, of course—the ones of the "I just don't want people to be embarrassed by me" and "I just want to be invisible" nature. But looking back, I've met every one of these, even the sad ones.

No, I'm not skinny, but that was never on the list, was it?

Whenever I'm feeling unhappy with my body or angry at myself for not treating it perfectly—when I'm feeling overweight, in particular—I must remember the main goal: to make sure my weight doesn't prevent me from living a full life. That is all.

!?

All the Body

I quit my job in part because it was giving me headaches. Well, guess what I've discovered? It wasn't my job that gave me the headaches—just like it wasn't my job keeping me from exercising, eating well, or being able to do the splits. I quit my job, and damned if I don't still have headaches.

I get migraines, and they start like this: I feel like there's a water droplet sitting on my left eyelid. The right side of my face starts feeling dulled and numb-ish. My gums start to feel weird, like I just put Baby Orajel all over them. My right ear feels stuffy, or sometimes it feels like my brain might blow out of my right ear. Hearing hurts, and the family must tip-toe, tip-toe, tip-toe around me like I'm a sleeping little princess. My brain starts doing weird tricks—like making lightning bolts appear out of nowhere. Or even cooler, if I put my finger in front of my face and move it from left to right, I can see the path where my finger has been, like that rubber pencil trick you learned in third grade. Somewhere in there I'll take a migraine pill, and like magic, all will go back to normal for a while—about three hours if I'm lucky—before the headache starts again.

A few rounds of this and then the migraine either goes away or decides it would prefer to stay a while. If it chooses to stick around, it'll camp out in my brain for weeks—sometimes months—and won't end no matter what I throw at it.

Sounds awful, doesn't it? But did you notice the one word I didn't use to describe my migraines?

Pain.

I'm one of the lucky migraineurs. I get pain-free migraines. Every once in a while I'll have a "real" migraine, but mostly it's odd stuff.

Before I knew these were migraines, I was sure I had a brain tumor (a super-sneaky one that could avoid detection on an MRI). I wouldn't take migraine medicine, of course, and left untreated, the phenomena went wild. I'd see spectacular light patterns, like an acid trip but without the fun. And I'd get vertigo. Awful, awful vertigo. Then there was the weird spatial confusion. When I was in a car, it felt as if the car was sitting still and the scenery was being pulled past me. When I walked, it felt like I was walking on a trampoline, with the ground giving way a bit with each step.

It took years for the docs to figure out what was going on. I was diagnosed with multiple sclerosis for a long while, and since I'm a woman, with anxiety. {Not that the anxiety diagnosis was incorrect—who wouldn't be anxious about visual hallucinations and dizziness? But it didn't get to the root of the issue.}

Finally, I got in with an MS specialist in Dallas, who within minutes concluded I had migraines. He connected me with a migraine specialist, who connected me with a neurotologist (a doctor who specializes in the ear-brain connection), and in two or three months they had me all settled. I still get migraines, but I can treat them quickly and aggressively. Best of all, now I know there's no brain tumor.

Apart from the migraines, things are picking up for me. I am finding myself less and less drawn to reality TV, more and more drawn to learning, and still not at all drawn to exercise. So yes, there is more work to be done, but I do think this project is helping me reenergize. But these damn migraines . . .

For this month, I've decided to focus on all things body. Since the exercise month—the body in motion—didn't take, perhaps focusing on the body at rest is a better idea. I hope you enjoy this knowledge of body. *{Get it? Knowledge of body? Instead of body of knowledge? I'm hilarious.}*

How Do These Shots Work, Anyway?

The doctor said monthly injections might relieve the migraines, and the strength of "might" was all I needed to reply, "Sure! I'll shoot that elixir into my body!"

I have no idea how these shots work. But this is learning-about-body time, so I get to figure it out! The problem? When I read about medical things, it's always laborious because I have to look up every third word. *{I have the same problem with recipes, since I don't cook at all. The minute the recipe says, "one cup boiled chicken," I'm off to research, because how long do you boil a chicken? Do you just throw it in boiling water or put it in a Ziploc or something? Do you toss it in cold water and then heat it up, to keep it from hopping out of the pot?}*

But sure, I'll give this a shot. *{Get it? I'm learning about shots. I'm going to give it a shot. Like I said, I'm hilarious.}*

Here's what I learned about these shots (and when you read this explanation, know that I took all of my college sciences at community college over the summer):

Your nervous system perceives outside stimuli and reacts to them as needed. It does this through nerve cells called neurons. Neurons pass electrical signals between each other so your body knows how to respond. One of the ways they pass these signals is through chemicals called neurotransmitters.

One type of neurotransmitter is called calcitonin gene-related peptide, or CGRP. It is a vasodilator, meaning it opens up the blood vessels so more blood can flow through. In people with migraines, the thinking (as I understand it, which is, well, unreliable at best) is that there's a brain dysfunction that causes CGRP to release. This dilates the blood vessels, which causes them to swell up and press on your nerves, at which point you're screwed.

The medicine I'm taking binds itself to the CGRP and keeps it from connecting with the receptor, so the vasodilation signal doesn't transmit. Think of it like a bouncer breaking up a fight by blocking the drunk from throwing punches. Another similar medication comes at it slightly differently, by blocking the receptor from receiving the signal—like a bouncer standing in front of someone, protecting him from the punches the drunk is throwing.

Thank you, scientists, for inventing this magic liquid that may calm my brain the heck down. Truly, thanks.

This One Makes You Taller

I also take other medications that are supposed to help with migraines. Thinking of those made me wonder why the two halves of a capsule are different colors.

Several reasons, I discovered:

- So pharmacists can distinguish one drug from another
- So patients, particularly elderly ones, can distinguish one drug from another
- So patients can see the medications against the background, should they be dropped

- For marketing purposes (based on customer preferences, brand recognition, etc.)

That makes sense. Honest to goodness, I have no idea what my pills are. I fill up four seven-day pillboxes, one month at a time. Once the pills are tucked in their boxes, I know that at night I take two small white ones, a red softgel, a big yellow capsule, and so on, but I don't recall what medications those are. I absolutely depend on color to notice what I'm missing.

So yes, it makes sense to me that capsules should be multi-colored—as should schools, workplaces, and the Oscars.

You Would Think He Wood Know
Rob told me he really needed to pee, as evidenced by, um, well, morning wood.

"Does needing to pee in the morning cause an erection?" I said.

"Yep," he said.

"Wow, I never knew that."

Also, I didn't believe it. I looked it up, because that's what I'm supposed to do during Project Couch to Curiosity.

The condition is called Nocturnal Penile Tumescence. It is not caused by needing to pee but by the increase in testosterone levels during sleep, with testosterone levels being at their highest immediately upon waking from REM sleep.

I reported this intel to my husband.

"Really? You fact-checked my penis?" he said.

"Well, yeah, but just so you know, I'm not one bit proud."

Spare a Penis?
Speaking of penises, when I was a kid, I lived in Guadalajara, Mexico, from the third to the eighth grade. Mama married

a guy who was a violinist in the Guadalajara symphony, in case you're wondering what took us down there.

I was telling Rob there were a ton of earwigs in Guadalajara, those little black insects with antennae on their heads and pincers on their tails. *{When you're talking about the antenna of the electrical variety, the plural is antennas. The plural of the animal antenna is antennae. How the hell did I not know that? That I also do not know.}*

"I was always worried the earwigs would crawl into my ears, lay their little eggs, and feast on my brain," I said.

"Do they do that?" Rob said.

Hmm, I don't know. Now I'm curious.

As it turns out, they don't, so all of my childhood terrors were unfounded—which would have been nice to know back then. If only Al Gore had invented the internet in the 1970s.

But I guess it's good I didn't know it back then, because then I wouldn't have looked it up and found this interesting fact: earwigs have a spare penis—an extra in case theirs pops off during copulation.

Can you imagine if men had an extra penis? Good god, they'd never let us rest.

Shama Lama Ding Dong

Still speaking of penises, I was talking to my friend Liz on the phone. She had just come back from a driving trip with her husband, David.

"David got sick of having to stop so I could pee every ten minutes," she said. "He kept telling me I should just pee by the side of the road like he does, but it's not as easy for women."

"It's just not fair. Men get all the perks in this world," I said.

"That's what I said! And then David said I should just get a female urination device."

"Female urination device—how have I never heard of that?"

"Hikers use them a lot," Liz said. "They're like pretend penises."

A female urination device is essentially a funnel with the tube of the funnel angled forward. You put the wide part over your hoo-ha, and then the tube part is your pretend penis. You can pee standing, like you're a dude. Of course, you'll want to be wearing pants with a long zipper, so you can place the funnel without having to pull your pants to your knees. These fake penises are generally made of reusable plastic or disposable cardboard (like the material of french fry containers). And Liz is right—they are largely marketed for use in hiking and backpacking.

I also discovered that there are female urinals. Some are urinals attached low on the wall (just above knee height), with long, narrow bowls. You walk up to the bowl, one leg on each side of the urinal, and face the wall. You simply stand and pee, though surely you have to squat a bit to avoid having pee drip down your leg. Other designs look more like toilets without the seat; you hover over the toilet like you would at any rest stop toilet, so what's the big design genius there? Either way, these seem impractical for those of us who aren't regular skirt wearers.

Here's my idea—and if you patent it and become a billionaire, I hope you'll remember me: pants with a zipper running front to back, from the top of your pubic line to the top of your arse crease. When you unzip, you really can stand and use a female urinal. Of course, you're going to have to figure out how to avoid the chafing and discomfort of having a zipper in your vagina, but that's why you're making the big billionaire bucks. {I just learned that these pants already exist. Damn, they were fast in stealing my big idea. There go your billions!}

87

Your Long Vagina

Speaking of vaginas, when I was looking up female urination devices, I decided I also needed a refresher on menstrual cups. Those may be all the rage now, but since I'm past the age of needing to care about menstruation, I don't know much about them.

Basically they are cups that you put in much like you would a tampon. You insert the cup folded, then somehow twist it, and it opens up like a spring flower. The cup collects your menstrual flow. You remove and empty it every six to twelve hours, depending on your flow.

Wirecutter had an article reviewing menstrual cups and picked the MeLuna menstrual cup as its favorite. Honorable mentions included the DivaCup, which *Wirecutter* selected as the best for "long vaginas."

What exactly is a long vagina? And how would I know I have a long one? Should I be measuring my vagina? If so, using what device—a ruler or a measuring tape? Where do I measure from and to? And why, oh why, am I measuring my vagina?

Questions like these make me so glad for menopause.

By the way, these penis and vagina learnings are all the rage among my friends. They're not all that interested in neurotransmitters and calcitonin gene-related peptides, but when I mention that female urination devices are made out of french fry containers, they lean in. Once they're hooked, I tell them about spare penises and vagina measuring, and they clamor for more, more, more. Try it on your friends. You'll see.

So Much Poo in You

Since we're talking about things below the belt, and since you could probably use more party conversation fodder, it seems appropriate that we learn a bit about colons.

My colon likes to grow polyps, small bumps of cells on the lining of the colon. Since they can develop into cancer, every few years the doctors do a colonoscopy and snip the polyps out. But before the harvest, there is MoviPrep.

Once, when I was stuck at home because of colonoscopy prep, my youngest son asked about the procedure, "Is that where you practice putting your fingers up your butthole?"

"Exactly," I said.

I think he might have been mixing up a colonoscopy with a prostate exam (not that you practice for those either), but where's the fun in clearing that up for him?

When these colonoscopy preps come along, I'm always amazed by how much poo I have in me. I'm curious how that much is possible.

Apparently your body produces one ounce of poo for each twelve to fourteen pounds of body weight. So that puts me at a little over a soda can worth of poo, which just isn't right because I had at least two liters come out of me during my last bowel prep.

I'd also like to know the difference between "poo" and "poop." I say "poo" most of the time, but every time I say it Rob corrects me.

"Did you mean poop?"

"No, I meant poo."

We have very highbrow talks, as you can tell.

It seems that the British prefer "poo." Americans prefer "poop." But don't tell Rob, because then he'll be all like, "We're 'Merican," and that'll just be annoying.

Let There Be Lights

Back to migraines. As I mentioned, when I get migraines, I often see lightning bolts. I turn my head to the left, and out of my peripheral vision to the right, *bang! {Except it's not the noise but the visual, so an onomatopoeic word might not have been the best descriptor.}*

Look down (like when I'm going down some stairs) and, *bang*, there it is again. Back when I thought I had brain cancer, or MS, or delusions, these hallucinatory weather phenomena were very concerning. Now that I know they are only migraine symptoms, they're just mildly disorienting.

I know these things are types of migraine aura, but what causes these ocular migraines (instead of all of the other weird symptoms I can get from a migraine)? Why does my brain choose to throw bright strikes all about me?

Unfortunately no good answers are available. I definitely have misfiring electrical impulses in my brain, but why those are creating a visual electrical storm and not an icepick-being-stabbed-in-my-brain headache, they don't yet know. But, boy howdy, am I ever thankful to have the weather pattern instead.

Sympathy Stroke

What if this time I'm not having a migraine but a stroke? What if this is really an aneurysm, and I'm going to die here on the kitchen floor in six minutes? Or what if, just maybe, I'm a hypochondriac and imagining all of this?

Oh good, a migraine pill made it all go away, so I guess I'm not nuts this time. I wonder if it's true that we women are diagnosed with hypochondria more than men, just because we're women. Or are we truly more fucked up than the men?

First thing I learned: They don't call it hypochondria anymore but somatic system disorder. Warning signs for somatic system disorder include things like the following:

- a history of going to a lot of different doctors, none of whose reassurance is calming

- being overly concerned about a specific body system or organ, like your heart or digestive system
- symptoms that shift or change
- a recent loss or stressful life situation, or a history of anxiety, nervousness, or depression
- symptoms that interfere with work, family, and social life

I absolutely do this. I'll decide my heart is crapping out on me, feel unheard by the doctors, finally convince them to run appropriate (or inappropriate) tests, then realize I'm fine. Never mind.

It took me a lot of years to realize that this was what my brain was doing. Now I know my pattern enough to either convince myself the problem is that I'm nuts or open my doctor's visit with the disclosure of my tendency to do this. Of course, I'm screwed if I really do get something serious wrong with me, because I've just reminded the doctors that I'm a little liar to whom they should pay no mind.

Anyhow, women are ten times more likely than men to report somatic symptoms. Why? Because somatic symptoms often occur with abuse or trauma, and women are more likely on the receiving end of that than men.

But aren't women also on the receiving end of "don't worry your little head about that" diagnoses? Yes, they are. Studies have found that women who report to the emergency room with pain are more likely to have a longer wait before being seen by a doctor, less likely to be classified as an urgent case, less likely to be given opioid painkillers, and more likely to be prescribed antianxiety medications and referred for psychiatric treatment. The role gender bias plays in medical treatment is just now starting to be defined, in part because before the creation in 1990 of the National Institutes of

Health's Office of Research on Women's Health, women were typically left out of medical studies.

So it's complicated, but we're still left with one central point: I do not have a brain tumor.

Sick and Tired

I just learned about two illnesses I have never heard of. Now I have two more illnesses to think I have. Hypochondria—I mean, somatic system disorder—expanded!

The first is thalassemia, which the Mayo Clinic describes as "an inherited blood disorder that causes your body to have less hemoglobin than normal." Because hemoglobin—red blood cells—carry oxygen to your body, thalassemia wears you the hell out. The word "thalassemia" is derived from the Greek word *thalassa*, meaning "the sea," because the illness was first identified in people living near the Mediterranean Sea.

Each of your parents contributes two genes involved. If you have one mutated gene, you'll likely have no symptoms but will be a carrier. If you have two mutated genes, you'll have mild symptoms. Three mutated genes and you're screwed. And with four, you were likely stillborn so won't be reading this.

Thalassemia can be cured only by bone marrow and stem cell transplant, though often it can be treated with frequent blood transfusions.

I don't have any of these mutated genes, as far as I know, yet I'm still worn out (thank you, menopausal sleeplessness!). Imagine what a mess I'd be with thalassemia.

The second illness is nontuberculous mycobacterial lung disease (NTM). This one will freak you out. It's a lung infection caused when you breathe in common bacteria found in water and soil. How do you breathe them in? Most commonly, from infected showerheads, steam rooms, or hot tubs where water droplets are aerosolized. Most people will be exposed yet never contract NTM. But folks who have asthma—like me!—are extra susceptible.

What are the effects of NTM? Like other lung infections, it can cause shortness of breath, fatigue, and chest pain. In severe cases, it can cause significant lung damage.

How do you avoid NTM?

- Stay away from hot tubs, particularly indoor hot tubs
- Use only filtered water in CPAP (sleep apnea) machines or humidifiers
- Avoid long, hot showers
- Regularly soak your showerheads with white vinegar or replace them regularly

Guess what I'm asking Santa to bring me this year? Showerheads. Oh, and I'd love a decent night's sleep if that's something Mr. Claus could wrap up for me.

Find Me a Diet
I need to go on a diet. Oh wait, I used the word "diet," when we're supposed to call it "a way of life." I can never get that right. Whatever it is, I need one.

This isn't one of those "I'm so faaaaaaat" things a skinny girl says. And it's not a body-shaming thing either. I mentioned in the last chapter that I had weight loss surgery. Here's a closer look at the path that took me there:

- I was a fat kid (though I'd kill to be that "fat" now).
- I lost weight in high school, through a combination of bulimia, weight loss pills (molly, I'm guessing, bought

All the Body

from some "doctor" in a dodgy strip mall), and boy angst.

- I gained—and I'm not kidding—eighty pounds in college, through a combination of pizza, beer, and lots and lots and lots more beer.
- I gained and lost and gained and lost until . . . three pregnancies, then I basically just gained from there.
- I got to just over three hundred pounds and then had a Lap-Band put in. It didn't work, making me further convinced the type of surgery I really needed was a lobotomy. *{And now that I wrote that word, I'm curious about lobotomies.}*
- After a year or so the Lap-Band was removed because it made me throw up all the time, and I feared my teeth would rot right out of my head.
- I gained and lost and gained and lost, until I had the gastric bypass. *{Head to "Just Keep Swimming" in the "All the Exercise" chapter if you missed it and want a little more info about these surgeries.}*
- I lost 160 pounds (which is like giving birth to twenty babies, eight pounds each, but without the perineal tear or the god-awful responsibility).
- I gained back about twenty-five pounds but was happy with that weight.
- I stayed stable for about seven years, then gained about forty pounds through a combination of stressful job, sapping work, and taxing employment.
- My gall bladder got wonky and made me sick, so I lost twenty-five pounds. *{Don't you just love it when you lose weight when you're sick? It's the best. When a friend tells me she had the flu, I always ask, "But did you lose weight?" And then she smiles and brags about how much she lost. Making lemonade, folks.}*

- I quit work, then lost fifteen pounds.
- I parked myself on the couch watching *90 Day Fiancé* and *America's Next Top Model* and gained five pounds.

I'm going to save you the math because I know you're going to do it anyway. That puts me at 170 pounds now. I'd like to lose about 10 pounds—down to 160—and stay in the 160 to 165 range. You may be sitting there thinking, "She's happy at 160?" Yup. What about it?

When thinking about what sort of food plan I next want to fail on, I start reading about gut microbiomes and how those might influence weight. I've always thought that with the way I eat, I should be about average-sized. But my body seems super-efficient at storing weight, which will serve me well in a famine or a Renoir painting but not so much otherwise. The articles I've been reading tell me one of the reasons for my poundage may be an unhealthy gut microbiome—and if I can balance and diversify the microbes in my gut, I might lose some weight.

Should I talk to my doctor about this? Suuuuuure. But in the meantime, I think I might eat more yogurt.

I Needed a Lobotomy

What are lobotomies, anyway? Do the surgeons cut out part of your brain? Do they cut pathways so the brain segments can't communicate with one another? Do they just blend it all up in there with a metal eggbeater?

I guessed it! They cut the connections between the prefrontal cortex and the rest of your brain.

What does the prefrontal cortex do? It's the executive function of your brain, responsible for things like focusing attention, predicting consequences, anticipating events, and filling out your damn taxes.

Whoa. That's a pretty important job. Take the prefrontal cortex away and it's like the toddlers in your brain are running the place. They'll have all the cartoons blaring, soda cans strewn about, and the adult scissors just sitting in the middle of the floor.

Lobotomies were all the rage in the 1930s to 1950s, used to treat schizophrenia, bipolar disorder, and other mental health disorders. In 1949 Egas Moniz was awarded the Nobel Prize in Physiology or Medicine for inventing the procedure.

The side effects of the procedure were severe, however. It had a mortality rate of about 5 percent. "Successful" outcomes resulted in lowered mental function, decreased emotional responsiveness, and confusion, making patients easier to control but forever altered.

By the 1950s, with the discovery of effective psychiatric drugs and the publicity of the procedure's negative outcomes, the lobotomy fell out of favor. Today it is considered barbaric.

Didn't one of the Kennedy kids have a lobotomy? Yes, Rosemary, sister of John, Bobby, and Ted. When her mother, Rose, went into labor, it took the doctor a while to get there. The nurses made Rose keep her legs crossed, keeping Rosemary's head stuck in the birth canal for two hours, deprived of oxygen. She was born with an intellectual disability that got worse over time. During her early twenties she started having seizures and violent mood swings. When she was twenty-three, her father, Joseph, had the doctors snip-snip her brain, without telling mama Rose that the procedure was being done. Oh. My. God. What a monster!

After the lobotomy, Rosemary couldn't walk or speak and was incontinent. She lived the rest of her life in an institution. Her mother didn't visit her for twenty years, and her father never came to see her at all. You see? A monster! And it sounds like Rose kind of sucks, too.

Okay, forget the lobotomy thing. I don't need one. Just a diet, please. Sorry, I meant "a way of life."

What Are Epigenetics?
I saw this headline in the paper: "'My 600-lb Life's Houston doctor reveals 22 weight loss tips in exclusive interview." Of course, I had to read.

Tip one: Blame genetics. Obesity is caused by genetics, along with epigenetics.

Oh great, the very first tip, and I'm already lost. I've heard the word "epigenetics," but I have no idea what it means. And when I go to look it up, I don't understand anything I'm reading, because as I've mentioned, my brain doesn't do science.

I Googled "epigenetics for idiots" and discovered that it's the idea that external factors—such as environment or diet—can activate or inactivate certain genes. Once those genes are lit up or turned off, you can pass them along to your kids.

Imagine pregnant, obese me. If I ate poorly during my pregnancy (oh no! I did), I could pass an instruction to turn on the obesity gene to my fetus, and I'M SO SORRY, KIDS, THAT I DID THIS TO YOU—I DIDN'T KNOW! *{But, kids, you also inherited the thick-hair gene, abundant in our lineage, so at least your thick thighs are counterbalanced. You're welcome.}*

Interestingly, it's not just pregnant women who can pass along these epigenetic markers. It is thought that the markers can be passed down generationally, so if great-grandpa ate poorly during his prepubescent years, the obesity marker could get turned on as his sperm developed and then passed on to tens of generations. *{Also interesting is that these epigenetic markers can be reversible. For example, some people have an epigenetic marker that turns off their tumor suppression gene.*

97

Cancer researchers have discovered targeted therapy to flip that switch and turn the suppression gene back on.}

So the first weight loss tip is telling me the genes I inherited, along with lifestyle influences I also inherited, might be to blame for my weight. It's not my fault. I just knew it.

Oh, and you're probably curious about the other twenty-one tips. They're bullshit. Basically, eat less, exercise more. Blah, blah, blah.

It's Hysterical, Really

Since my retirement, we've been spending more time at the cabin in the Texas Hill Country. I got my pup, Miley, a dog bed for outdoors. It's basically a rectangular flat cot on legs that elevate it about six inches off the ground. It's made of nylon and weighs three pounds tops.

Miley was confused by it, as she is by all new things, and eyed it with suspicion. With encouragement, she stepped up on it but put all of her weight awkwardly on one side. The bed tumped over on top of her. {What does "tump" mean? Oh, that's Texan for "tip or turn over" and such a useful word that I can't believe everyone doesn't use it. The world should also be using "y'all" (which means "all of you"), "all y'all" (which means "each and every damn one of you"), and "bless her heart" (which has far too many nuanced meanings to review in this book).}

Rob was up on the deck when this went down. He sprung, making it over to lift the lighter-than-her-dog-bowl cot off of Miley in a cool 1.2 seconds.

"Wow, Rob. I think you saved her life," I said.

"Yes, yes I did," he said. "I like to use superhuman strength and speed for all nonemergency situations."

I'm curious about this superhuman strength. Is that really a thing? Could you really lift a car if your child were under its wheel?

The phenomenon is called hysterical strength. A few things I found interesting:

- You can't really lift the full weight of a car, even in a life-or-death situation. At most, people can lift a few hundred pounds (though that could be just enough to get one corner of the car slightly off the ground).
- How much you can lift in such situations depends on your muscle strength. Ordinarily your body protects itself by having you use a maximum of about 60 percent of your top muscle strength. Hysterical strength situations might get you up to 80 percent.
- Your body puts limits on the use of your top muscle strength through pain and distress signals. In emergency situations, your brain ignores those signals, allowing you to use more of your muscle strength.
- In emergency situations, your body releases adrenaline, which increases your breathing and heart rate. This sends a boost of oxygenated blood to your muscles, making them more fully recruitable.

Hysterical strength is thought to have allowed a mother in Quebec to protect her children by wrestling an eight-foot tall, seven-hundred-pound polar bear. Hysterical strength is thought to have allowed a construction crew chief to lift a fifteen-hundred-pound crashed helicopter to free its trapped pilot. Hysterical strength is thought to have allowed Rob to lift an airy canvas cot that had gone off kilter and almost (but not quite) brushed our muscly Labrador.

Here's the learning: the next time your beloved pet has a piece of light nylon fall on her, your husband may well overreact, so stay out of the way.

!?

All the Animals

Now that I'm home during the day, Miley has been stuck to my side, and I have grown even more attached to her than I was already.

Sure, Miley has her faults. You can't really take her for walks because she's afraid of people, moving cars, parked cars, fluttering leaves, wind gusts, and unexpected spots of shade. It's tough to take her to the dog park because she's afraid of other dogs—in that they engage in motion and come with scary owners. She doesn't like to go outside, even for bathroom breaks, for a few days after the lawn guys have been here, on the off chance that they might return. Basically, Miley is a neurotic mess of a rescue dog. But I'm a neurotic mess too, so I'll be darned if I'll cast her out for it.

My renewed love for Miley has inspired me to make animals my next focus of learning.

I'm six months out from retirement now, and I feel like I'm rocking along quite nicely. Yes, I had quite a few migraine days last month, and those held me back. But overall I'm having fun learning new things. Have I yet found purpose in my learning? Not exactly, but isn't the learning purpose enough? Couldn't

I spend my life skittering between things I'm curious about, with no end goal? Couldn't I pretend I'm a college student whose only job is soaking in knowledge while hung over?

I say yes. Psychology says maybe.

Erik Erikson was a German American psychologist who in the mid-1950s posited that humans have eight stages of psychosocial development. At each stage they encounter a psychosocial crisis that they must successfully resolve in order to have a healthy personality.

Stage	Age	Description	Virtue achieved when stage is successfully reconciled	Result of failure to reconcile
1	Birth to 18 months	Trust vs. mistrust	Hope	Withdrawal
2	18 months to 2–3 years	Autonomy vs. shame/doubt	Will	Compulsion
3	3–5 years	Initiative vs. guilt	Purpose	Inhibition
4	5–12 years	Industry vs. inferiority	Competency	Inertia/ passivity
5	12–18 years	Identity vs. role confusion	Fidelity	Repudiation
6	18–40 years	Intimacy vs. isolation	Love	Distantiation
7	40–65 years	Generativity vs. stagnation/ self-absorption	Care	Rejectivity
8	65 years to death	Ego integrity vs. despair	Wisdom	Disdain

Given that I'm smack dab in the forty to sixty-five age range, these stages tell me I should be focused on generativity—that is, establishing and guiding the next generation, taking care of others, being productive, being creative, and doing things that make the world a better place. Erikson tells me that if I succeed in making it through this stage, I'll likely feel that I have been useful in my life and contributed to society. If I fail, I'll feel disillusioned and disconnected from the world.

I feel generally good about where I am in this stage. I went through my forties raising and nurturing my children, whom I'm confident will meaningfully contribute to society (well, I'm confident about them on most days). I spent much of the last few years of my work life training younger folks, helping them learn how to think about and address workplace issues. And now I'm focused on being productive with learning everything about everything (or something about a lot of things, anyway).

Erikson tells me that the trick to avoiding stagnation and moving on to stage eight, where I will look back on my life and feel as if it had integrity and meaning, is to keep up the productivity, creativity, and service-mindedness. I'm moving in the right direction, but I need to keep chugging along.

I know I'm not there yet. Hell, I'm still having a hard time explaining what I'm doing with my life. Here's a recent example. I ran into a woman who falls somewhere between acquaintance and friend. I've known her for years and we keep up with each other through social media, but we're not "talk-on-the-phone friends." {Her husband and I made out once. It was back in college, well before she and he connected. He was a sloppy kisser, all tongue and liquid. So we're "kissed-the-same-guy friends" but definitely not "talk-about-what-an-awful-kisser-he-is friends."}

Acquaintance/friend: I heard you retired! That's so exciting!

Me: Yeah, it's pretty sweet.

Acquaintance/friend: So what do you do all day?

Me: Nothing really.

Acquaintance/friend: How nice! But really, what do you do all day?

Me: Try to avoid conversations like this one.

I laughed—awkwardly, like I do. She stood there still expecting an answer.

Me: Not much, really. I'm just trying to learn stuff. Like if I don't know a word, I look it up. Or if I don't know something, I read about it. Or something. Like about animals. I'm going to learn about animals now. So not much. Except learning some, I guess. Or something. Yeah, not much. Animals.

Acquaintance/friend: Looking up words and animals. Ah, that sounds just lovely.

I wanted to reply, "Your husband slobbers when he kisses, and it's disgusting," but I restrained myself. She already knows that, don't you think?

Long May She Live

Here's how Miley came into our lives. When my youngest son, Clark, was in eighth grade, he was emotionally flat. He wasn't so much depressed as disinterested. At some point Rob said, "You know what? He needs a dog." That was about the craziest thing Rob could have said, because at the time we were contemplating retirement and had big travel plans. But I knew he was right. Clark did need a dog.

Clark had a dog at his father's house—a basset hound named Wally. But when his dad and second wife got divorced, the dog went with her and Clark lost his dog. Clark missed the companionship.

As it happens, our local dog rescue had a dog available with the very same name as the one my ex's second wife got in their divorce—Wally. Rescue-dog-Wally was an overweight beagle, so he even looked a bit like the second-wife-stole-my-kid's-dog-Wally.

We went to meet rescue-dog-Wally but soon discovered that he was a fifteen-year-old tired lump who had no interest in meeting Clark. The dog rescue folks said, "You really should meet Miley." Miley was a seven-month-old yellow Labrador retriever, all tongue and paws.

Clark was still tied to the memory of second-wife-stole-my-kid's-dog-Wally and couldn't decide which dog to take. In my not-best-parenting moment, I asked, "Do you want to take this dog, who is old and going to die soon, or this cute puppy who loves you?"

The decision was made. Miley came home with us and stuck by Clark's side for about a year. They were in love. Then, as teenage boys do, Clark pulled out of his funk. His calendar became full of social plans, and Miley was left on her own, so then she stuck by my side for about a year. We were, and are, in love.

This morning as I was looking at her across the room, I thought, "She had better not die." And then I realized she will definitely die, and I thought, "Oh gosh. When is she going to die?"

Answer: The life expectancy of Labradors is ten to twelve years.

If the math is seven dog years per human year, she'll live the equivalent of age seventy to eighty-four. Except that's not the math, because the whole seven-dog-years thing is completely made up. Instead, most dog experts look at dogs in stages rather than years. The American Animal Hospital Association describes the five life stages of a dog:

> **Puppy.** Lasts from birth to when the dog stops growing rapidly, usually six to nine months.
> **Young adult.** Lasts until the physical and social maturing stops, usually at three to four years.
> **Mature adult.** Lasts until the last 25 percent of estimated life span.
> **Senior.** Lasts until end of life.
> **End of life.** Lasts until, obviously, the end of the dog's life.

So Miley is a mature adult, even though she acts just like a baby when someone turns on the vacuum, rings the doorbell, or blows their nose—waking from peaceful slumber to demand comfort. Thank God she doesn't know about nursing, because that would be just gross.

Long May I Live Too

Miley is going to live a while, but what about me? A study I read said having a dog helps you live longer. You have a 24 percent risk reduction of all-cause mortality with dog ownership. Oh, yay, a 24 percent greater chance I won't die—ever! Or do they mean I'm less likely to die on any given day? Or in any given year? I mean, it's good news no matter what it means, but I'm curious.

Apparently a lower risk of all-cause mortality means a lower risk of death during the follow-up period of the study, whatever that may be.

This dog study was actually a review of prior studies on the effects of dog ownership. When you look at all of those studies, over all of their follow-up periods, in general you were 24 percent less likely to die during the study period if you had a dog and 31 percent less likely to die of a cardiovascular event. That's pretty sweet.

Why are dogs such life-givers? The thinking is that having a dog makes you more active (which just isn't true for me because my laziness trumps my dog's desire to go for a walk), lowers your blood pressure (more dog petting, less stressing), and helps with loneliness and depression (dogs are the best company).

So hug your dogs, folks! It's good for you!

P.S. I love you, Miley.

Here, Horsey

I was on a flight recently and my neighbor had a cat stored under her seat, like it was a purse or something—except I'm not allergic to purses. I mentioned it to Mackenzie.

"Maybe it was a service animal," she said.

"A service cat?" I said.

"Sure. All sorts of animals can be service animals, even miniature horses."

I was suspicious, so I looked it up.

She's somewhat right! The Americans with Disabilities Act regulations limit service animals to dogs (so she's wrong about the cat thing). But the regulations were revised to add miniature horses if they are individually trained to help the disabled person (so she's right about the horse thing).

Facilities don't automatically have to let miniature horses in, though. In deciding whether to accommodate, the facility may consider the size and weight of the miniature horse, whether the handler has control of the animal, whether it is housebroken, and whether its presence would compromise safety.

But do you have to stuff the horse under the airplane seat, or do you carry it in your lap for takeoff and landing? Or maybe you just stuff it in the overhead bin? Nope, it has to sit on the floor in front of your seat.

The miniature horse made me wonder what happens if you're allergic to animals. Do airlines have to accommodate your allergy by keeping animals off of your flight? Like that cat my neighbor brought with her? Not that I dislike cats. I used to have cats, until I got pregnant, my asthma got out of control, and the OB made me choose between the baby and the cat. I hesitated a bit but ultimately made the right call (I suppose).

Yes, airlines have to accommodate your allergy, but they can do that by moving your seat or moving you to a later flight.

What if the animals on board your particular flight are not service animals (that is, not ADA-protected)? If your allergy is of sufficient severity to constitute a disability under the ADA, is the airline then required to kick the pets off your flight?

Generally not. The thinking is that there is always animal dander on planes—on people's clothes, and so on. If you're so allergic you can't be around animal dander, then you shouldn't be on planes at all. And if you're just a bit allergic, well, your allergy is not a disability.

Okay, all good intel. But I still don't want that dander-y cat seated next to me.

Fear Factor

As I mentioned earlier, our dog is afraid of people. When we first got her, Miley would pee when she was scared of someone. A sweet neighbor came up to pet her? Crouch and pee.

All the Animals

One of the kids brought a friend over? Crouch and pee. She became aware of another human being in a neighboring zip code? Crouch and pee.

Miley has gotten better. Now she barks and trembles instead of crouching and peeing. But I'm curious. Is there something I could be doing to help her?

The internet has the following ideas:

- The ThunderCap. This looks like the blinders they put on carriage horses, except it fully covers the dog's face. At first I thought it completely blinded the dog, which seemed unworkable. But apparently the dog can see through the blindfold, though dimly. This product gets bad reviews on Amazon, like this one: "My girl was able to get this off in fifteen seconds." *{Oh wow, they put this on their girl? No wonder it didn't work. I believe it was intended for dogs.}*
- Treats. Some suggest giving the dog treats whenever the threat heads her way. I get that this could work, but would I not be rewarding, and thus encouraging, the fearful behavior?
- Exposure therapy. Some folks suggest exposing your dog to all things scary until she gets over it—except Miley hasn't gotten over it in years, so now what?
- Comfort. Some say when the dog shows fear, you should comfort her instead of reprimanding her, by petting or massaging her, reassuring her everything will be okay. That's a fine idea, but read on.
- Never comfort. Other folks say whatever you do, you should not comfort your dog when she shows fearful behavior, because this confirms that there is something to be feared and reinforces the behavior you are trying

to get rid of. Great. Definitely comfort her but never comfort her.

- Avoidance. Some suggest simply keeping your dog away from things that scare her. That's crap advice. I'd have to keep Miley in a dark box to avoid everything that frightens her.
- Drugs. Some suggest giving your dog antianxiety medication. That seems to make sense. Meds sure work to quell my anxiety. If dogs take on the characteristics of their owners, no wonder Miley's a wreck. Pretty soon she'll be drinking too much wine too.
- Switch and bait. Finally, some suggest teaching your dog a wanted behavior—for example, bring me a beer. You then reward your dog whenever she runs to get you a brew. You get your dog fully trained to the command, then start using it when the fearful situation comes up. That seems to make sense. Miley would then "brew me" instead of "crouch and pee." Though I think they probably have a different command in mind, like "watch me" or "sit" or something. But then who would bring me my flippin' beer?

Which idea did we try? Switch and bait, for about three days—just long enough for us to decide prematurely that it wasn't working and was a hassle besides.

You Big Ol' Schnauzer

Rob took Miley to a dog park. When he got home, he announced, "Miley's throwing up." And he wasn't kidding. She threw up all evening long. She didn't want to eat dinner, so of course my I-like-to-catastrophize mind jumped straight to stomach cancer. She was dragging her head, and then she

All the Animals

sprawled on the cold bathroom tile. I was sure she was going to die. You'll be glad to know that this morning, she's fine. Cancer cured!

Anyhow, we were talking about the dog park, and Rob mentioned that one of the dogs there was huge and looked like a giant schnauzer. He asked if I knew what kind of dog that could be. That's the perfect sort of learning for Project Couch to Curiosity!

As it turns out, the breed that looks like a giant schnauzer is called "giant schnauzer." How perfectly descriptive.

I also learned that schnauzers are in the working group. I wouldn't have guessed that. I thought schnauzers were terriers. In the 1800s in Bavaria, schnauzers were farm dogs used primarily to drive livestock to market. They were also good at herding, retrieving, and guarding, so they were all-purpose helpers.

As schnauzers were needed less on the farm (with machines taking over their duties), they were increasingly used as guard dogs. Since bigger is better in a guard dog, schnauzers were bred with Great Danes, rottweilers, and Dobermans to make the fearsome giant schnauzer.

Wouldn't it be fun to assign humans to groups, like they do with dogs? Are you herding, sporting, nonsporting, working, hound, terrier, or toy? I don't like getting people organized, so herding's out. I don't love hunting and fishing stuff, so sporting is out. Truth be told, I can be selfish and sometimes not the best helper, so working is out. I'm not known for my great sense of smell, so hound isn't an option. I'm not overly energetic, so out goes the terrier group. And I'm certainly not toy-sized. I guess that means I'm in the nonsporting group of humans—like a human French bulldog.

And you?

All Things Mouse

I was talking to a friend who is a word geek like me.

"She's such a sweet pup," I said of Miley.

"Mouse or dog?" my friend said.

"What?"

"Pups. Those can be mice or dogs."

"And you're wondering why you don't have a boyfriend?"

Sure enough. Baby mice are called pups or pinkies. How the hell did I not know that? Female mice are does, and males are bucks.

I also learned if you take a mouse pup away from its mother early, you need to feed it kitten or baby formula with an eyedropper (makes sense) and stimulate its bowels with a Q-tip (the fuck?). If you don't do the anal rubbing, the baby mouse won't go to the bathroom and presumably will become a swollen poop ball.

Mice are cheap to buy, in case you're curious—about five bucks each. Feeder mice (bred for feeding to snakes) are even cheaper—like a buck fifty. You can buy a whole bag of frozen mice for about a buck each, if you're so inclined.

I am not.

Poisoning the Puppy

Have I mentioned that Rob is a wonderful cook?

It's possible he smoked a bit of pot in his younger years.

It's possible pot is associated with a lack of motivation.

It's possible a lack of motivation has an impact on continued educational opportunities.

It's possible a lack of continued educational opportunities can result in parental financial disassociation.

It's possible parental financial disassociation can lead to restaurant work.

It's possible early age exposure to restaurant work can lead to superior cooking skills.

It's possible superior cooking skills can make your later-in-life wife very appreciative.

So yay for teen pot smoking!

Anyhow, last night's feast: shrimp and green beans with almonds. Perfectly healthy for me, but what about for Miley? She asked and asked for a bite, but I hesitated. Can dogs eat shrimp? Is that safe?

Yes, dogs can eat shrimp if they're cooked, shelled, and given in moderation. But while I'm at it, here's what they can't eat:

> Chocolate. Yes, we know, but did you know no coffee or tea either?
>
> Booze. Seriously? Who does that—gives up their beer, I mean?
>
> Raw bread dough. The yeast can rise, distending the dog's stomach.
>
> Apple seeds. They have cyanide. Whoa.
>
> Avocados. They contain persin, a fungicidal toxin, which dogs are usually somewhat okay with, but it causes diarrhea. The main problem with avocados is the choking hazard, so no pits for puppy. That means no persimmons either, folks.
>
> Grapes and raisins. They can cause kidney failure.
>
> Xylitol. So no candy, gum, mouthwash, or toothpaste.
>
> Macadamia nuts. In case you're visiting Grandma.
>
> Onions, garlic, shallots, chives. These damage red blood cells.
>
> Dairy. Oh good, because I did not want to share my ice cream.
>
> Fat trimmings. Ewwwww.

Bones. They splinter.

Raw eggs. Unless your dog's name is Rocky?

Mushrooms. They cause shock and death. Oh shit,
that's bad.

Salt. Sodium ion poisoning, whatever that is.

So what can you feed your dog? Dog food. Don't get complicated.

Oh, and while we're talking about poisoning your dog, I once poisoned Miley—accidentally, of course. I brought home a bag of chocolate protein shakes and bars. She chewed up all of the bars and bit into the shake boxes. I called poison control. They told me to give her hydrogen peroxide, which works like ipecac does for humans. Of course, she wouldn't drink it (probably because she was all full up on protein bars), so they had me soak bread in hydrogen peroxide. She ate that, and then, well, let's just say the threat passed.

Okay, Okay, Already

My editor tells me I need to diversify and talk about cats for a change.

I don't have anything against cats. As I mentioned, I used to have cats, until I got too allergic.

But even people who have cats don't have a lot to say about cats. They're cute in videos?

That's really all there is.

Dark Duck

When we were at my brother's house for Thanksgiving lunch, he gave us some duck. He's a hunter (because male + born Texan = hunter), so he keeps duck in his freezer like I keep ice cream—except I don't keep ice cream in the freezer because I already ate it.

I got to wondering why duck breast is dark meat while the meat of chicken and turkey breasts is white. And why are chicken legs dark meat but breasts white?

Dark meat is caused by myoglobin, a protein that carries oxygen to the muscles and is reddish in color. Because chicken and turkeys stand on their legs, their legs are heavily muscled, full of myoglobin, and thus dark. Because chicken and turkeys are flightless, their breasts have fewer muscles and thus less myoglobin, making their breasts white meat.

But ducks do fly, so their breasts are muscular and full of myoglobin and thus dark.

Reading my scientific explanations is like taking Science for Nonscience Majors. You might not get scientifically accurate information, but it's an easy A.

Eat Shit!

The first time Rob and I woke up together on the first of a month, and I greeted him with "rabbit, rabbit" instead of "good morning," he was worried about what he had gotten himself into.

"You've never heard of rabbit, rabbit?" I said.

"I have no idea what that even means," Rob said.

"On the first day of the month, your first words should be 'rabbit, rabbit.' Then you'll have good luck for the rest of the month. I guess because rabbits are lucky."

I have other good luck tricks. Whenever there is a thrice repeating number or letter on a license plate, I touch red and say, *¡Feliz encuentro!*, which means "Happy encounter!" or "Happy finding!" in Spanish. When I see a pink car, I cross my fingers for good luck and keep them crossed until I see a dog. And I would never, ever cry on New Year's Day, knowing a single tear could bring a year of sadness.

I also know better than to toast with water, but I have no idea why that would bring bad luck. What's the thinking there?

It's a Navy tradition, with the lore being that toasting with water would cause the person you are toasting to die by drowning. Well, wine it is, then!

Back to rabbits though. I heard that rabbits eat their own poop, and I'm curious about that.

Poop-eating, or coprophagia, gives rabbits a second try at getting the nutrients out of food sources. Rabbits have two different kinds of poop—one meant for eating and one not. The noneating kind of droppings are called fecal pellets and are primarily undigested fiber. The eating kind are called cecotropes and contain healthy bacteria that are reintroduced to the digestive system and are an essential part of the rabbit diet.

Since I like to bring everything back to dogs, there's a clever trick to keep your dog from eating her own poop, if she's inclined to do that. Feed her a few pieces of fresh pineapple (or as an alternative, Adolph's Tenderizer, which contains pineapple). The pineapple contains an enzyme that makes the poop taste bad so the dog will leave it alone. Of course, this suggests that the poop tastes good without the pineapple, but we're not going to think about that.

Tsk, Tusk

A neighbor in San Antonio has a set of elephant tusks prominently displayed in his front window. Thankfully, I've never met this neighbor. Why thankfully? Because I'm guessing he's a big game hunter, and I don't have a lot to talk about with big game hunters. He's not necessarily a game hunter, I suppose—but remember, I live in Texas, so yeah, he's definitely a big game hunter. He didn't necessarily kill the elephant himself, but I'd bet my farm (if I had one) that he thinks killing elephants for their tusks is good sport.

I thought having an enormous set of elephant tusks prominently displayed in your front window was illegal. Just the sort of thing I should be learning this month.

It's not illegal. US regulations do not prohibit personal possession of elephant ivory, but only the buying and selling of it. The elephant killed to make the enormous set of elephant tusks prominently displayed in the neighbor's front window is already dead, so regulating the display of its tusks would not help bring the dead elephant back to life or protect other elephants from poachers.

There are exceptions that allow you to buy and sell elephant ivory within the United States:

- Trade within your state, if you can prove that the ivory was imported before 1990.
- Items qualifying as antiques under the Endangered Species Act, which stipulates that they be more than one hundred years old, not repaired or modified with more ivory or any part of a protected species since 1973, and imported through a qualified port.
- Items fitting within the de minimis exception, which is less than 50 percent ivory by both volume and value, less than two hundred grams of ivory, and imported into the United States before 1990.

What about importing from outside the country? Importing ivory for commercial purposes is completely forbidden. For noncommercial purposes, you may be able to import sport trophies, inherited items, or musical instruments, if the ivory contained in them is from an animal removed from the wild before 1976.

A few other interesting things I learned:

- Elephant tusks function as the elephant's incisor teeth and have nerves, tissues, and blood vessels running the length of them, much as a tooth would.
- Elephants do not regrow their tusks.
- Just as a human is right- or left-handed, an elephant will have a preference for use of its right or left tusk.
- An elephant's tusks are embedded into its skull, so poachers carve the tusks out of the elephant's skull to retrieve them.
- Likely as an evolutionary response to poaching, about 50 percent of elephants are now born without tusks. Scientists are studying the impact of tusklessness on elephant behavior patterns, including whether tuskless elephants have larger home ranges out of a necessity to cover more land to find food.

Tsk, tsk to my neighbor for having tusk, tusk.

Fur Baby

It confuses me when people call their dogs their fur babies. It often sounds like a defensive move—like "No, I don't have any human babies, but I have these here dogs, and I love them as much as you could possibly love your children, so back off."

Do you know who should be defensive? People who have children but don't let them have dogs. That's just criminal.

Moving on from that, did you know some dogs have fur and some have hair?

Dogs with a single coat are said to have hair. Dogs with a double coat—that is, a shorter, denser, and more shed-dy undercoat that insulates and a softer, longer, less shed-dy topcoat that repels—are said to have fur.

All the Animals

So which dogs have fur? The bushy ones you'd expect, like the Welsh corgi, chow chow, German shepherd, Newfoundland, and husky.

But which one didn't I expect? Labrador retriever. Which explains why Miley sheds all over the damn house.

Poor Clark. Miley sleeps in his room, so he has it the worst. Everything is his room is furry—the sheets, the rug, the toothbrush. When he puts on his navy sweatshirt to go off to school, the poor kid looks like a chia pet.

Perhaps we should brush Clark from time to time.

A Herd of Cows

I invited a friend to come out to my cabin this weekend. While we were there, the cattle on the neighboring property were mooing.

"What is a group of cows called?" she said.

"You aren't from Texas, are you?" I said.

She's not. And in the event you aren't either, a group of cows is called a herd.

But here are some other animal collective nouns I did not know:

- Apes: Shrewdness
- Bears: Sloth or sleuth
- Buffalo: Gang, herd, troop, or obstinacy
- Crocodiles: Bask
- Ferrets: Business (What do you call a gathering with apes, buffalo, and ferrets? A business of obstinate shrews.)
- Flamingos: Stand (That one is apt.)
- Frogs: Army
- Giraffes: Tower (Also apt.)
- Gorillas: Apt (The most apt.)

- Hippopotami: Bloat
- Lemurs: Conspiracy
- Parrots: Pandemonium (Yup.)
- Porcupines: Prickle (Genius!)
- Rabbits: Procreation (Just kidding, it's a herd.)
- Rhinoceros: Crash
- Skunk: Stench (Now the namers are just getting lazy.)

Wow, that's a whole collection of collective nouns I didn't know. And here I've been using "fuck-ton" all of these years.

!?
All the Music

Since I quit work, I've stuck pretty close to home. Rob and I decided it was time for a trip, so we went to Taos for a music festival. We met two other couples there. These couples aren't just any friends. They're smart, engaging, grade-A friends. These are friends who support me when I am at my worst, when all I can talk about is reality television. And they're friends who celebrate me when I'm at my best, when I'm my chattery, clever-comeback-y self.

Guess what version they got this weekend? Yes! My best! I was filarious! (Translation: fucking hilarious.)

I was telling them about this project and how much fun it has been to engage my brain. Sure, I learned a lot when I was still working, but it was all about things I was required to learn—case law, regulations, blah, blah, boring. Now I can learn about female urination devices, how to unboil an egg with urine, and how baseballs were once made of horse foreskins. These are the sorts of things my friends don't get to learn about in their jobs, so they wanted me to teach them everything.

All of which is to say, this project is doing for me exactly what I had hoped—transforming me from a couch-adhered zombie to an engaging storyteller—and that feels wonderful. I've been thinking about what I'd like my next focus to be. Since the month kicked off with a wonderful music festival weekend, it's only fitting that it be music. So I will pay particular attention to all things tonal. I anticipate a harmonious month.

Keep It Simple, Stupid

Going to the music festival inspired me to want to play a musical instrument. But which instrument is the easiest for a musically challenged person?

The internet consensus: ukulele. It has only four strings, which makes it easier than the six-string guitar or the eight-string mandolin. And the strings are nylon, so they're easier on the digits.

Most people put piano as second choice.

The hardest instruments to play are said to be violin, French horn, and organ—violin because it has no frets, requires bowing, and demands multitasking; organ because it has no sustain pedal so notes must be held to sustain sound and because it requires both keyboard playing and foot-pedal pushing; French horn because the notes are so close together and because it is less forgiving than other brass instruments.

It occurs to me that I could ask the question of my singer-songwriter sister Edith. Edith is signed to the Drag City record label out of Chicago, has released seven studio albums and EPs, and has songs featured in movies like *High Fidelity*.

When I asked her which instrument you can learn to perfection in about five days, she didn't seem too annoyed by my question and concluded that I should consider a mountain dulcimer, a stringed lap instrument that looks like a long, narrow guitar, has three to five strings, and a fretted fingerboard. To play, you rest the dulcimer in your lap and strum it with your right hand with a pick or quill. You push down the strings on the frets with a noter (a popsicle-stick-looking piece of wood or bone), held in your left hand.

Edith explained that the mountain dulcimer is easier than the ukulele. Since you have the instrument in your lap, you can see what you're doing. The melody is played with only one string. The noter makes it easy on your fingers.

I looked online and, yeah, I think I'll consider the dulcimer. I like the way it sounds. You can catch me on stage once I become expert on it—in a week or two. *{Except I didn't become expert in it. Why? Because I spent days looking for the perfect dulcimer to buy and somewhere in the middle of all of that research, I got distracted. By what? Who knows. It could have been anything—a marital discussion, politics, the blender.}*

They Say It's Your Birthday

If my son Clark could eat every meal at Chili's, he would. I keep telling him that man shall not live on Honey-Chipotle Chicken Crispers alone, but he's out to prove me wrong. I caved to his preference for dinner tonight.

While we were at Chili's, we got on the topic of the restaurant chain's original birthday song.

"What's the deal with that?" Clark said. "Why don't they just sing the regular happy birthday song?"

"It has something to do with copyright stuff," I said. "I'll look into that."

I learned that the song has an interesting story to it. But first, some legal-schmegal background you need to know about how long the copyright on a song lasts.

If a song was created or first published in 1978 or later, the copyright lasts seventy years after the death of its author (longer for anonymous works or works made for hire). If the song was published or registered before 1978, the copyright lasts seventy-five years from the date of registration or the date of publication with a copyright notice. But there's an exception: the copyright is extended to ninety-five years for any song whose copyright had not expired as of October 27, 1978.

The birthday song has been the subject of quite a copyright battle. The tune was written in 1893 by school principal Patty Hill and her sister Mildred, who sang the song as "Good Morning to All" for kindergarten students. The happy birthday lyrics were attached to the tune and first published (but not registered) in 1912, without a copyright notice.

In 1935 the Summy Corporation (later purchased by Warner/Chappell Music) registered the song, listing its authors as Preston Ware Orem (who did one of the piano arrangements) and Mrs. R. R. Forman (who wrote a second verse to the song). This registration started the seventy-five-year clock on the copyright. The copyright would have expired in 2010, but because the copyright had not run out as of October 27, 1978, it fell within the exception and was entitled to twenty additional years of protection— through 2030.

In 2015, however, a federal judge ruled that the copyright owned by Warner/Chappell applied only to the specific piano arrangement of the song, not to the tune or lyrics.

Up until that year Warner/Chappell had reportedly been charging up to $10,000 for permission for the song to appear in film and earning royalties of approximately $2 million a year on it. In 2016 the company agreed to pay $14 million to settle claims for prior royalties collected. The court approved the settlement and officially declared the song as public domain.

So I will say without having to pay a penny for it:

> Happy birthday to you
> Happy birthday to you
> Happy birthday to I Don't Know What Your Name Is
>   Who Is Reading This
> Happy birthday to you

I reported back to Clark that Chili's could now sing the regular happy birthday song without having to worry about paying royalties.

"If I got royalties from Chili's, I'd make them pay me in Chicken Crispers," Clark said.

Of course he would.

Cover Me

The happy birthday song is in the public domain, but what happens when people sing songs that aren't? I know you have to pay royalties to the songwriter if you record their song. *{Interestingly, permission isn't required, just payment. Why? In 1909 Congress passed the Copyright Act, which provided a "compulsory license" allowing songs to be used, provided a licensing fee was paid. In passing the law, Congress aimed to undercut the efforts of the company Aeolian to corner the market on player piano music by buying up song licenses from musicians and publishing companies.}*

What if you just perform it? If you are an artist and cover someone else's tune in a live show, do you have to pay royalties for that? I'm curious.

The answer: Yes, but the live venue owner usually takes care of that by getting blanket rights from the performing rights organizations (ASCAP, BMI, and SESAC). A song-writer or publisher who keeps their catalog up to date with these performing rights organizations (PROs) is then paid for each cover of their song.

So if there's a blanket license, how do the PROs know you have covered a song? A few ways:

- You submit your set list to the PROs. What's your incentive? You get paid for playing your own songs (and any artists you cover will get paid because you played their tunes).
- Some of the larger music venues are required by contract with PROs to submit set lists of those who play at their venues, so all of the songwriters get their share.
- PROs survey the set lists of all the major concert tours throughout the country. If you're a superstar musician, anyone you cover will get paid that way.
- PROs do samplings of other live music venues. If your set is part of that sample, then you may get paid that way.

I fact-checked this with my sister Edith. She told me the reality is that neither musicians nor venues submit set lists very often. She explained that PROs are not really chasing down payment for live performances, but they do make sure venues playing background music have blanket agreements in place so musicians can get paid through sampling at those venues.

As a songwriter, you make your real royalty money from sales and downloads of your music (mechanical royalties), radio play (performance royalties), and TV or film play (sync fees). And by real money, I mean "a very tiny amount of coin" for most songwriters—barely enough to cover the cost of your weed.

I'm in a Field of Poppies

Speaking of weed, I am so tired—field-of-poppies tired. I don't know if I'm getting sick or if this is just the after-effects of anesthesia. Yesterday I was given a drug called propofol—commonly called "milk of amnesia" because of its milky appearance and memory-wiping ability—for a minor procedure I had. *{Okay, okay, it was a colonoscopy. Geez, do you have to know everything?}*

It's odd to think that Michael Jackson had himself hooked up to a propofol IV every night so he could sleep. I know it killed him in the end, but I just don't understand how he could function on the days he *didn't* die. One day of that smack in my veins and I could barely keep my eyes open.

Speaking of Michael Jackson, wasn't there something about him patenting his shoes? Was it so he could do the moonwalk?

No, the shoes he patented allowed him to do the lean-forward antigravity move seen in his 1987 "Smooth Criminal" video. Jackson was attached to wires to achieve the move in the video. But in order to recreate the lean for his live shows, he patented shoes with a slot on the bottom. A peg rose from the stage into this slot, holding the shoes onto the ground. Lean shoes have been around for ages (and were used widely by circus and vaudeville performers), but with the shoe anchor invention Jackson could lean to 45 degrees (whereas the most someone could lean without anchoring would be about 30 degrees and that's with a trained dancer's core strength and conditioning).

And then he hooked himself up to a propofol IV and died, when he could have just gotten a colonoscopy instead.

The Captain's Daughter

One great thing about this project is the genuine excitement I feel when I discover something I don't know. Before Project

Couch to Curiosity, a knowledge gap might be an annoyance (Grrrr, I don't have time to figure this out), an embarrassment (Oh, God, how can I be over fifty and not know why the sky is blue?), or a hypochondriacal crisis (I think I might have early onset dementia. In fact, I'm sure of it. Have you noticed me forgetting things? I'm forgetting things, aren't I? Did I already ask you this?). But now, it's a serotonin jolt (Oh, yay—something to learn!).

I take joy in discovering any little thing I didn't know. But when it's about my specific focus for the month? Absolute glee. But sometimes my glee seems misplaced.

Example: Rob was singing the drunken sailor song, the "What shall we do with a drunken sailor . . . Way hay, and up she rises" one.

"Put him in the bed with the captain's daughter, put him in the bed with the captain's daughter, put him in the bed with the captain's daughter, early in the morning," Rob sang.

"That seems kinda rapey," I said.

"What?"

"Saying you should put the drunken sailor in bed with the captain's daughter."

Rob explained that the captain's daughter is not a girl, but a whip—a cat-o'-nine-tails. As punishment, a misbehaving sailor in the Royal Navy would be whipped, covered in saltwater (ouch!), then put to bed.

"That's wonderful!" I said.

Rob shook his head and walked into the other room.

Luckily, Rob is aware of the project (obviously), so he knew the source of my excitement. But I need to remember to be careful with others—not to exclaim but to casually note the new learning, like it's no big thang, and jump up and down later in the privacy of my home, where the only person I'm confusing is Rob.

All the Music

Trumpet or Bugle?

I'm guessing you're sitting there wondering about the difference between a trumpet and a bugle. Funny you should ask, because I just looked that up. I also found out about the cornet for you, because I'm nice that way.

First, the bugle. It doesn't have any finger valves or holes, so there are limited notes (only five) you can play. You change the note by changing your mouth shape (called embouchure). You make higher notes with a tighter lip and faster air. You make lower notes with a looser lip and slower air.

Trumpets have finger valves, so they are able to make more notes. If a valve is not pressed, the air goes through a hole in the valve and out the other side. When a valve is pressed, the valve diverts the air through a different, longer tube. The longer tube length allows for lower notes. Each valve engages a different tube length, allowing for differences in sound.

A cornet looks like a small trumpet but with a more tightly coiled tube.

The metal tube, or bore, of the trumpet has the same diameter from the mouthpiece to the valves (called a cylindrical bore). The cornet's tube increases in diameter (called a conical bore). Because of these differences in shape, cornets have a warmer tone, while trumpets have a clearer, sharper tone.

As I mentioned, I don't play any instruments, not even the ever-so-simple dulcimer. My mother made me take piano lessons when I was little, but I stopped after "Robin sitting in a tree, won't you spend some time with me." Maybe if the songs hadn't been so idiotic. Who wants to spend time with a damn robin?

Ring Ring Ring

I have another migraine. {*Are these migraines getting tedious for you? Yeah, I feel ya. They're tedious for me too. Maybe even a little more tedious for me than for you.*}

My head feels like a tuning fork. It actually makes the high-pitched tuning-fork hum, and that hum vibrates down my neck into my right shoulder. I've tried to figure out what key it's in, but it's multi-tonal, so it's difficult to identify.

This American Life did a piece once about a guy who had ear ringing (tinnitus, they call it), with a different, noncompatible note in each ear. He was always wanting the sound to resolve, with one pitch moving up to harmonize with the other, but the sounds remained off. The story made me thankful that when I get headaches, only one of my ears gets angry and noisy.

So now to learn something from this. What's the difference between pitch and key? I use them interchangeably above, but I know they have different meanings.

Pitch identifies how high or how low a sound is, which is determined by how many sound vibrations are made per second. Low sound = few vibrations. High = many. This frequency of vibrations is measured in Hertz, abbreviated Hz. {*No relation to the rental car company, which was named after owner John Hertz.*}

A note is a particular pitch. For example, a frequency (that is, sound vibrations per second) of 440 Hz will make the same sound as the A above the middle C on a piano keyboard.

A scale is a group of notes that are commonly used together—do-re-mi-fa-so-la-ti-do (called the solfège scale), for example.

The key is basically the home or main note your piece of music is based on. So if you're in the key of C, you could sing the C note throughout the piece and it wouldn't clash with the other notes in the song.

If you're singing off-pitch, you're singing the note either sharp or flat—right note but you're a little off. If you're singing off-key, you've picked the wrong note entirely.

And if you're me, you sing both off-key and off-pitch at the same time, and there's no resolving those sounds.

Harry Potter Piano-y Thing

What is the piano-y instrument with bell sounds played in "Hedwig's Theme" in the Harry Potter movies? I wonder not because I want to play one but because I'm curious, like I can be.

It's a celesta, and it looks like a child-size upright piano. It does not have strings like a piano; rather, the hammers hit against metal plates to make sound.

It's also the instrument used in the *Nutcracker*'s "Dance of the Sugar Plum Fairy" and, surprisingly (to me, anyway), in *Mister Rogers*'s "It's a Beautiful Day in the Neighborhood." It's also played in Rod Stewart's "Maggie May," but darned if I can hear it no matter how many times I listen.

More Instruments

I heard folk, bluegrass, and Americana musician Rhiannon Giddens on NPR. She mentioned clawhammer banjo. I got a little knowledge-gap adrenaline jolt.

What is a clawhammer banjo exactly (or inexactly, which is the type of understanding I'm going for)?

With a clawhammer style (also called trailing), you curl your hand like a claw and use the thumb and index finger to pick out a melody. You then strum downward with the backs and fingernails of your other three fingers. Clawhammer is an older style and has an older sound to it.

Clawhammer is supposedly easier to learn than three-finger- or bluegrass-style playing. With that style, you do not strum at all but use the thumb, index, and third finger and pluck in an upward direction. You pluck more notes, so the sound has more depth, but the melody can get lost in all of those notes if you don't know your stuff.

I won't be learning either style, though, because banjo is dang hard and I'm dang stupid. Well, on instruments anyhow. I'm smart about other stuff. Like what? Ummm, sudoku, maybe?

Annie, Get Your Music

I learned an interesting story that is tangentially related to music.

I have a copy of Annie Leibovitz's book *At Work*. Seeing the cover made me recall something about her losing the rights to all of her photos.

In 2008 and 2009 Leibovitz borrowed $24 million from Art Capital Group, using her real estate and the rights to her photographs as collateral. She is said to have used the funds to pay for home renovation costs, to settle tax liens, and to pay for lawsuit settlements.

In July 2010 Art Capital sued Leibovitz for breach of contract, alleging that she had failed to repay the debt and had refused to cooperate with the company on the sale of her real estate and photographs.

Leibovitz resolved the matter with Art Capital after securing a $40 million loan from Colony Capital to refinance the debt. As part of the refinancing, Leibovitz regained control of her photographic rights.

Whew. It's sad to think of an artist losing rights to their artistic works. Some jerk could get the rights and use them in ads for handguns, hemorrhoid cream, or unnecessarily gendered products (baby wipes for girls!).

But then, while I was looking up information about Leibovitz's financial issues, I read that she photographed John Lennon on the day he died. How did I not know that?

Biography.com provides the following timeline:

11 a.m.: Annie Leibovitz arrives at the Dakota apartment building. She photographs John

Lennon and Yoko Ono for *Rolling Stone* magazine. One of the photos she takes is the iconic photo of a naked John on the bed, embracing a clothed Yoko. *{Seriously, how the hell did I not know that photo was taken on the day he died? That's heartbreaking.}*

12 p.m.: A friend of Lennon's meets David Chapman outside the Dakota. Chapman tells the friend he is hoping to get John to autograph a record (*Double Fantasy*) for him.

12:40 p.m.: RKO Radio employees arrive at the Dakota for a radio interview.

4:30 p.m.: John and Yoko exit the Dakota with the RKO Radio crew. Chapman approaches John with the record in hand. While John signs the record for Chapman, John's friend photographs the two. John and Yoko then get into a limousine, which takes them to a recording studio.

10:50 p.m.: John and Yoko return to the Dakota. Chapman is waiting outside. He shoots John four times with a .38 handgun. Within minutes John is taken to Roosevelt Hospital.

11:15 p.m.: John is pronounced dead.

Chapman pleaded guilty and was convicted to twenty years to life. He remains in prison.

The various reasons he has given for the assassination include the following:

- He was seeking fame and attention.
- He was angered by Lennon saying the Beatles were "more popular than Jesus Christ."

- He was incensed by Lennon's song "Imagine," which he saw as phony, in that Lennon preached about imagining you have no possessions while Lennon himself was wealthy.
- He was envious of Lennon's lifestyle.
- He was inspired by Holden Caufield in *Catcher in the Rye*, who derides phoniness. On the day of the assassination, Chapman was carrying the book, in which he had inscribed, "This is my statement."

As Paul McCartney so inelegantly worded it after hearing of the murder, "Drag, isn't it?"

Poliolio

Did you know that both Neil Young and Joni Mitchell had polio? Rob was listening to Neil Young music, which made him look up Young's backstory, which led him to the polio thing.

"How the hell did I not know that?" Rob said.

"Hey, that's myyyyyyyy line. You stole my line," I said.

"Oh yeah, sorry."

Joni Mitchell got polio when she was nine years old, during the epidemic's last hoorah in Canada. She credits the polio with the start of her interest in music, when she sang Christmas carols while isolated in the hospital.

Neil Young got polio in summer 1951, when he was almost six years old, during the same polio outbreak in Canada. His song "Helpless" makes reference to the mandatory isolation of infected households during the polio epidemic with its lyrics, "The chains are locked and tied across the door." *{In 1976 Young performed the song when he joined the Band for their final show. During his performance, he had a huge cocaine booger that had to be edited out by director Martin Scorsese before the release of the concert film* The Last Waltz.*}*

How does a person get polio? The CDC website says that it is contracted from "contact with the feces (poop) of an infected person." I love the (poop) parenthetical. Some scientist actually had to write that (shit) because they were afraid people would think feces is hair or something.

The Brown Note

And since we're talking about (poop), I recently heard of something called "the brown note"—a sound lower than humans can hear, somewhere in the 5–9 Hz range, rumored to cause a human to defecate.

Scientific experiments haven't borne out the theory though. *Mythbusters* did a "brown note" experiment and declared it a myth busted.

I'm glad my kids didn't know about the mythical brown note. As it was, they used their iPhones to play a high-frequency sound (in the 17,400 Hz range) that teens can hear but adults cannot because ear cells die off with age. The kids would play the tone, look at each other, and start giggling, while I was left wondering what was so funny.

Apparently some city parks blare that high frequency through the night, using a device called the Mosquito, to keep teenagers from loitering.

It's a shame the brown note is just a myth. If it weren't, they could use a Brown Note Mosquito instead. If all the loitering teens shit their pants, that would pretty much put an end to loitering.

You're the Top

Ever wonder how the band ZZ Top got their name? Well, I did, and now you're going to find out, whether you like it or not.

Founder Billy Gibbons was in his apartment pondering a name for the band. He noticed two posters on his wall—one for B. B. King and one for ZZ Hill. He liked the ZZ, and since B. B. King was the "tops" as musicians go, he decided to go with ZZ Top.

Some added info that is going to make you feel old—and you are welcome to turn the page or put down the book if you are not in the mood to feel that way: All three of the band-mates in ZZ Top were born in 1949. The band was formed in 1969. That means they're older than seventy, and the band has been around for more than fifty years. And now I want to cry.

But here's something that cheered me up. In 1984 Gillette offered Billy Gibbons and Dusty Hill $1 million each to shave their beards. They turned it down, saying they would look too ugly without the facial hair. {The third member of the band, Frank Beard, doesn't have a beard, funnily enough.}

Plaster Caster

I saved this musical tidbit for the end of the chapter, because it's my favorite.

Do you know about Cynthia Plaster Caster? She was an artist (real name Cynthia Albritton) famous for cast-ing molds of the erect phalluses of musicians. She got her start in 1968 when she was given an art class assignment to cast a solid that could retain its shape. Somehow she per-suaded Jimi Hendrix to play along, and a career was born. She later cast the erect penises of Jello Biafra (Dead Kenne-dys), Aynsley Dunbar (Journey), Dennis Thompson (MC5), Eddie Brigati (Young Rascals), Keith Moon (the Who), and Noel Redding (the Experience), among others.

How did the process work? Typically, Plaster Caster oiled up the musician's member so it wouldn't get stuck in the cast. Then a helper (or the musician's wife or girlfriend, or some-times the artist herself) got the musician aroused, often by oral stimulation to the phallus (such a fancy phrase for blow job). While things were getting steamy, Plaster Caster mixed up the alginates, the same molding material used for dental molds. When the material was ready, the musician stuck his member into the mold. The helper continued to stimulate the subject indirectly so he stayed hard. The penis stayed in the mold for about one minute, until the material hardened.

Seems risky. What if the material hardened in such a way that a guy's penis was trapped? He'd be stuck going to the hospital with a plaster cast stuck on his privates.

"No, really, this is for an art project," he'd say to the doctor.

Since learning about Cynthia Plaster Caster, I've told many people about her.

"What are you doing with your life these days?" someone will ask.

"Did you know an artist named Cynthia Plaster Caster cast the erect phalluses of musicians?" I'll say.

That's why sometimes people go out of their way to avoid me.

‼️

All the Texas

As I've mentioned, I have a small cabin in the Texas Hill Country. The real estate listing promised that this property would provide total seclusion, privacy, and comfort, and it has. It takes fifteen minutes from when I first hear a car coming to its arrival. I lose cell service when I'm about thirty minutes from the place. And it takes service providers at least forty-seven days to make their way to me for any household emergency. It's good living.

When I first quit work, I didn't much want to leave the house, but now Rob and I have been spending more time in the Hill Country. The place is equidistant from three state parks, so we do a lot of hiking. We stargaze. We go in search of swimming holes. *{Water is hard to come by in Texas, so it's always a scouting mission.}*

Spending time out here reminds me how much I love Texas. Not that I ever forget (Texans seldom do), but it renews my fervor, I suppose you could say.

Rob—who is originally from Upstate New York, spent most of his adult life in Virginia, and didn't move to San Antonio until 2006—has gotten accustomed to Texas, but without the birthright he'll never quite understand my passion. He often reminds me how much other Americans hate people from Texas. I asked him to explain why, and he had answers.

"Well, let's see," he said. "You're all Republicans and super-religious."

"I'm liberal and fairly skeptical," I said.

"Yeah, but in general Texans are right-wing zealots."

"Okay, is that it?"

"Oh no, there's lots more."

"Like what?"

"The state slogan: 'Don't mess with Texas.'"

"That isn't a state slogan. It was an antilittering campaign."

"Well, it has become the slogan. Shall I continue?"

"No, I'm good."

He has a million other beefs with Texans, like how they're always talking about secession, how they have refrigerator magnets in the shape of the state, how so many of them are televangelists, how they always speak of the state as the biggest and best, and how they don't know how to drive in the rain.

Rob can say what he will about the state, but where does he live? Texas. Where will he retire? Texas. Where will he probably die? Texas. This place has a certain draw.

What exactly is the draw? So many things, but I love the diversity in particular—of people, of geography, of experience. Want to drink margaritas and listen to mariachis? Come to San Antonio. Hike and stargaze? The Texas Hill Country. Bay fish and beachcomb? Head toward Corpus Christi. Or maybe you're more into wide open spaces. Head to West Texas and Big Bend. Fancy cars and makeup? One: Sorry we can't be friends. And two: Jet to Dallas. A fan of traffic and oil companies? Houston. {Houston people at least are nice, but I'd rather meet them in Austin for the weekend.}

I love that the culture of the state is one of friendliness. Texans say hello, hold doors open, and are kind to each other. Yes, it would be a little more friendly if the state were less red (okay, a lot more friendly), but it's moving in that direction.

And don't even get me started on the music—the sweet, sweet Texas music (shout-out to Austin here—hey, y'all!). Willie, Waylon, Beyoncé, Lyle, Stevie Ray, Selena, Townes, and on and on and on.

Besides, Texas is the biggest. And the best. So yeehaw. And to celebrate that, I'm going to make learning about my dear, beloved Texas the focus for the month.

Roadkill Cuisine

"What do we do if we find a dead animal on the property?" Rob said. We're out at the cabin, and we're definitely city folk who don't know how things are done out here.

"Kick it over to the neighbor's property," I said.

"But one that's not kickable, like a deer or something large."

I didn't know, so I looked, and here's what I found out. You call the game warden, and the warden will guide you. I'm sure I could have found a more specific answer if I felt more industrious. But looking this up has made me curious about something else: What if you find a dead animal in the road? Can you eat it?

Some states say roadkill can be on the menu, but not Texas. And you can't tag the dead animal and pretend you shot it either. If you find it on the road, you may drag it to the roadside if it's blocking your path. Otherwise you should leave it be. The Texas Department of Transportation will pick it up on their rounds.

And now you want to know where you can eat a wrecked deer, don't you? Alabama, Alaska, Arizona, Arkansas,

California, Colorado, Georgia, Idaho, Illinois, Indiana, Maryland, Massachusetts, Michigan, Missouri, Montana, New Hampshire, New Jersey, New York, North Carolina, North Dakota, Ohio, Oregon, Pennsylvania, South Dakota, Tennessee, Utah, Vermont, Washington, West Virginia, and Wisconsin. *As per normal, I can't figure out what is going on with Florida. They used to be a roadkill free-for-all. They're not on the roadkill cuisine lists anymore, so I figure some law changed, but darned if I can find it. A friend told me that Florida made harvesting roadkill illegal after too many folks were running down gators to avoid hunting regulations, but I haven't been able to confirm. So if you're chowing down on roadkill in the Sunshine State, best do it under the cover of darkness.}*

Just don't peel it off the asphalt and say, "But Lucie told me I could!" There are restrictions in many of those states, like licenses, permits, tags, notifications, and animal inspections.

Damn, now I'm hungry.

Don't Cross the Purple Paint

Like I said, many of the ways of rural Texas are mysterious to me. This trip I've noticed a lot of fences with posts painted purple. Why is that?

A purple-painted tree or fence post means "no trespassing."

By Texas law *{and maybe other states' laws too. This month I'm focused on my great state. Sure, I could consider yours, but that'll have to be for another month.}*, the paint mark has to be at least eight inches tall, one inch wide, and three to five feet off the ground. And you can't just paint one tree in the corner of your property. You have to put the paint marks one hundred feet apart on forestland (that is, land with trees that are potentially valuable for timber) or one thousand feet apart on unforested land.

Tell the kids about this when you're driving through Texas. It'll keep them busy and quiet for a good seven minutes. Okay, three.

Thirty to Fifty Feral Hogs

Whenever I'm in the Hill Country, feral hogs are a topic of conversation. There are many hogs in the area, and when I come to the property I can see evidence of them. They root, leaving long troughs in the ground. I have yet to see them in person, but I know they're watching me.

I mentioned something about the thirty-to-fifty-feral-hog meme to Rob, and he had no idea what I was talking about. Here's the backstory, in case you missed it too. After some mass shootings in Dayton and El Paso, musician Jason Isbell tweeted, "If you're on here arguing the definition of 'assault weapon' today you are part of the problem. You know what an assault weapon is, and you know you don't need one."

Some guy replied, to the world's delight, "Legit question for rural Americans—How do I kill the 30–50 feral hogs that run into my yard within 3–5 minutes while my small kids play?"

A meme was born. The visual of small kids in the backyard surrounded by all those feral hogs and the daddy coming outside and making a bloodbath of it all—ohhhh, people just loved it.

This left me wondering about the difference between a feral hog and a wild boar. Here's the best answer I found: Wild boars have always been wild. Feral hogs were once domesticated but are now wild. Boars and feral hogs have bred in the wild, so now you just have a whole mishmash of big ass swine out there.

Beware.

What about javelinas? How are they different from feral hogs and boars?

Hogs, boars, pigs, and javelinas are all in the same order of mammals—Artiodactyla, or even-toed ungulates. What's an ungulate, you ask? A hoofed mammal.

You may remember from middle school science class (I didn't) that orders are broken down into families, families into genera, and genera into species. Hogs, pigs, and boars are in the same family—the Suidae family, often referred to as old world pigs. Javelinas are in the Tayassuidae family—new world pigs.

Javelinas—the common name for collared peccaries—look somewhat like hogs but are smaller, don't have a visible tail, and have smaller ears. Honestly, I've been looking at photos, and I'm not sure I could tell the difference if one were charging me—except feral hogs weigh two hundred pounds on average and javelinas weigh fifty pounds or so. So yeah, I could tell the difference.

By the way, every time I hear the word "javelina," I think of a song by a Dallas comedy troupe from the 1970s and 1980s, Bowley & Wilson, which went something like this: "Lucy's got a poosey like a javelina hog, oompah, oompah, pah, pah." And now you will too. You're welcome.

Paint by Embers

I went to lunch with Mama. Her partner, Craig, is writing a book profiling Texas artists. One of the artists Craig is profiling made his art with unclaimed cremains. The artist would go down to who-knows-where-you-go-down-to and ask for any leftover cremains they have, mix them up, and then voilà—art! The creepiest thing? He put the name of the dead people on the back of the paintings.

I discovered that unclaimed cremains are a big problem for funeral homes. Family members will decide they can't or won't pay for the cremains and never pick them up. *{Unsolicited business tip for funeral homes: prepayment.}*

Or the family doesn't understand that cremation isn't the last step of the process, perhaps thinking the relative gets totally burned up when cremated. Anyhow, funeral homes end up with extra cremains.

Sometimes the funeral homes will bury the unclaimed cremains. Some states let funeral homes donate them for medical research. Many states let the funeral directors do what they want with them, once the cremains are unclaimed for a prescribed period of time.

Here's the most important thing I learned from all of this: the artist's name, Wayne Gilbert from Houston, Texas. If you feel the need to dash to the internet, you are excused.

The Sails of Braille

I took my youngest son, Clark, to the doctor. A mom and her daughter were sitting in the waiting room. The mom started talking to another woman about school starting and other mom chat.

"I don't have to buy school supplies for my daughter," the mom said.

"Why is that?" the other woman said.

"She goes to a special school. They provide all the supplies."

"That's convenient."

"Yes, all of her materials are in braille."

"Is learning braille hard?" the other woman asked.

"Not too bad. I'm trying to learn it myself. Braille is basically like dominoes, with three sails," the mom said.

Dominoes I get. We have lots of dominoes in Texas. But three sails? What does that mean?

I researched it, and here is what I discovered—that all Texans need a translator. Braille is not dominoes with three sails. It's dominoes with three *cells*.

Each braille cell is a grouping of six dots, set up in two columns of three each—just like the number six on a die. Each letter is made by using a combination of those six dots, as indicated on the figure below.

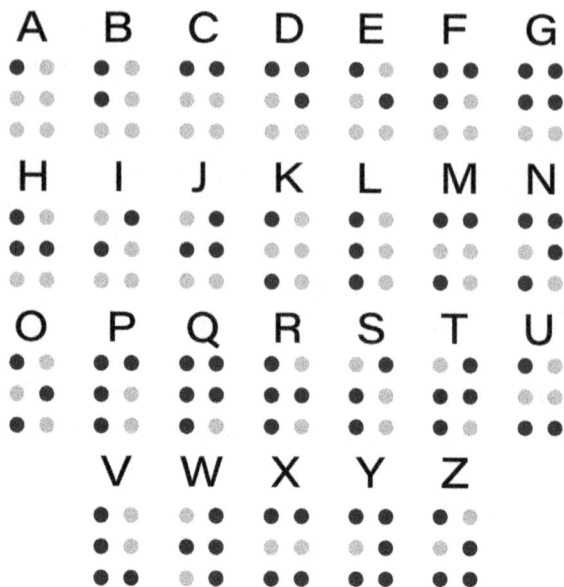

A B C D E F G

H I J K L M N

O P Q R S T U

V W X Y Z

- The first ten letters (A–J) are variations using the top four buttons.
- The next ten letters (K–T) are exactly the same, but they add the bottom left button.
- Skip W for now, because it wasn't part of the French alphabet when braille was thought up by Frenchman Louis Braille.
- The next five letters (U–Z) add the bottom right button.
- And W is just screwy so you'll have to figure that one out on your own.

Okay, that learning wasn't really about Texas, but since it required deciphering the Texas accent, I think it counts, don't you?

Is Your Turgid State Discernable?

Summer is always fun for sane Texans, because we get to see what crazy-ass laws will come into effect on September 1. In the year of Project Couch to Curiosity, 2019, our legislators spent time passing a law protecting kids' lemonade stands and another allowing beer and wine delivery on Sundays. But my favorite: kitty key chains are now legal!

What are kitty key chains, you ask? They're like brass knuckles (which are also now legal), but in the shape of a cute kitten for the little ladies. I guess the thinking is that if you can carry an assault rifle down the street . . .

Another favorite: Sending unsolicited dick pics will be against the law in Texas and punishable by a fine of up to $500. House Bill 2789 prohibits sending pictures of sexual conduct, exposed intimate parts, and covered male genitals in a "discernibly turgid state," unless sent at the request of or with specific consent of the recipient.

I gotta say, I feel a bit sorry for the guy whose turgid state is not discernible.

Beware the Sixth Dildo

While learning about turgid states (isn't retirement learning grand?), I also discovered that Texas law technically prohibits you from having more than five dildos. I say "technically" because the law has been declared unconstitutional and thus wouldn't be enforced, but it is still on the books.

The Texas Penal Code on Obscenity says it's a state jail felony to promote (or possess with the intent to promote) any obscene material or obscene device. And what's an "obscene device"? A device including a dildo or artificial vagina, designed or marketed as useful primarily for the stimulation of human genital organs.

And now the fun part. The Texas Penal Code goes on to say, "A person who possesses six or more obscene devices . . . is presumed to possess them with intent to promote the same."

Beware the sixth dildo.

Yeehaw! Back to School!

September is also fun for parents because it's back-to-school time! Sure, sometimes that's a pain because you have to start worrying about bedtime and homework, but it's pure gold for me this year because Clark got his driver's license! So this morning, did I wake up early to make him breakfast? Nope. Snooze. And I can get away with it, because "I'm helping him grow into independence." See how that works?

Of course, school starting means I'm now broke, because I just spent several hundred on school uniforms. How do most people afford these? My son has to wear not just any khakis but khakis from one particular uniform store. And since there are limited sizes in stock, we have to order the pants and then take them for alterations, thus the several hundred.

Turns out the Texas Education Code has worked this out for folks. School districts are required to set up uniform funding for "educationally disadvantaged" students, defined as those who participate in the free or reduced-price lunch program. Well, that's one thing the Texas education system got right. One.

One bad thing about back-to-school time is that there's more public parenting to be done. I will have to attend Back-to-School Night, show up for school performances, and have awkward small talk with other parents. It's that last one that saps my strength. I wish they'd have special seating at these events for the grouches, where we could just read our books in peace.

I See a Bad Moon Arisin'

An ongoing life theme is how stupid I am for a smart person. I regularly discover things I should know but don't.

This weekend at our Hill Country cabin we were having trouble seeing the stars because the full moon was being an asshole and ruining the skies for us. Rob suggested we go to bed early, then set an alarm for 4 a.m. Friday morning, once the moon had set.

"What does that mean?" I asked.

"What does what mean?"

"Once the moon has set."

As he scrunched up his face in confusion, it dawned on me.

"Oh yeah, I guess the moon does set, but it had never occurred to me," I said.

All fifty-plus years of my life, even knowing that Earth rotates and all, I imagined the moon sitting up there in the sky waiting for the sun to go down so it could shine.

Most of you are probably thinking, "How, how, how did she not know that? Is this a failure in our educational system? Just plain stupidity? Early onset dementia?"

But there are a precious few of you—and folks, you are my people—who are thinking, "I guess I knew that? But how does it work, really? Sure, orbit or something. But how exactly?"

So even though this has nothing to do with Texas except I thought about it while in a cabin deep in the heart of Texas (clap-clap-clap-clap), it's a nice time to explain a bit more about our shining ball of cheese.

Let's start with this. It's not made of cheese, which I'm guessing you knew. And it's not shining at all. Remember? The moon only looks bright because the sun is shining on it.

Now let's talk about the phases of the moon. The moon spins on its axis, just like Earth does, though more slowly. It takes about a month for the moon to make a full turn on its axis (vs. Earth's twenty-four-hour axis spin). The moon orbits Earth, just like Earth orbits the sun, though more quickly. It takes about a month for the moon to orbit Earth (vs. Earth's one-year orbit around the sun). Because the moon is spinning on its axis and orbiting Earth at about the same speed (approximately one month), and because Earth exerts a gravitational pull on the moon, the same side of the moon is always facing Earth.

Here's a handy graphic to show you what I'm talking about.

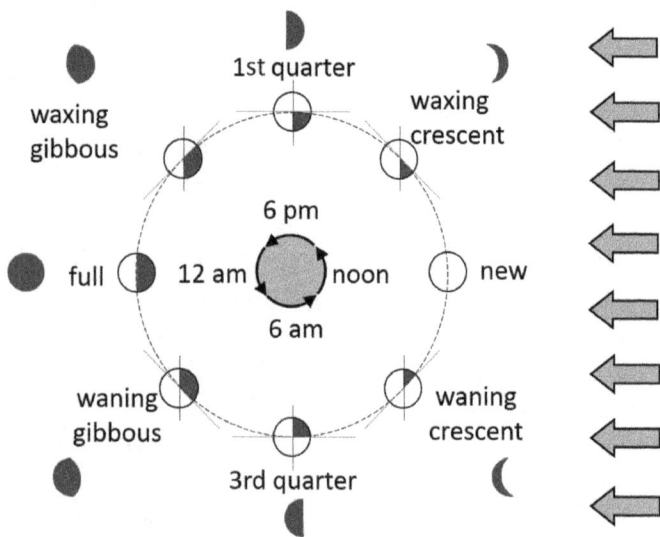

Earth is in the middle here. The moon is circling Earth. The arrows at right are the sunlight. The longest line skewering the moon at each phase indicates the half of the moon facing

Earth. The shorter, vertical line skewering the moon at each phase indicates the half of the moon illuminated by the sun.

When the sun illuminates only the half of the moon not facing Earth, the moon is not visible to us. That is called the new moon. When the sun fully illuminates the half of the moon facing Earth, we see the moon as a full moon. Throughout the month, as the moon orbits Earth, more or less of the moon will be illuminated by the sun, which is what gives us the lunar phases.

The major phases of the moon—new, first quarter, full, third quarter, new—happen approximately seven days apart from each other.

With me so far? Cool. Then on to why the moon rises and sets.

Remember when I said Earth spins on its axis every twenty-four hours? That's why the moon rises and sets—essentially, we're spinning past the moon, which changes where we see it in the sky.

Now I'd bet you're wondering, "But doesn't the moon spin too?" You are a clever one, aren't you? Yes, but because the moon takes about a month to spin on its axis, that doesn't have much of an effect on where we see it in the sky—some, but not all that much.

I'm done with all of the knowledge I can get without actually having to build a little solar system out of Styrofoam so I can visualize. And that, folks, I will not do.

Run the Traps

"I'm not sure who is going to be where for Thanksgiving," I said to Rob.

"I thought they were coming to our house," Rob said.

"I don't know. Mama and Daddy at the same table? I'll have to run the traps on that."

"Run the traps? What does that mean?"

All the Texas

149

"I don't really know, actually. You've never heard that phrase?"

"Never."

"I think it has something to do with hunting. Maybe it's when you go set off all of the traps so whoever is running through won't get caught in them?"

Rob got to searching on his computer. "The internet says it's checking the hunting traps to see what you caught in them."

"You really never heard that phrase?"

"Nope."

So, here's my question: Is this a regional, Texas thing?

I'm guessing yes, so let's go with that.

I know that's not a researched answer. I must confess that I've struggled a bit this month. I was zipping along so nicely during the music month, but now I'm trudging through Texas.

This retirement thing is harder than I predicted—going from fully scheduled days to nothing, from daily hits of great-job-Lucie affirmations to nothing, from being something to being nothing.

Right now, I'm a parent, yes, but my youngest will be headed off to college soon, and then what? Besides, I'm actively trying to "mother" less to get him ready to be off on his own. So now my role in life is to look up little factoids? That's my purpose? Really?

Shit. I've got to figure this out. I'm so privileged to have been able to retire this young. I'm so privileged, period. And now I'm whining about it? Ugh.

Remember the Alamo

As I said, I was rocking along so well last month, and then all of a sudden I began to wonder if I was spinning my wheels with Project Couch to Curiosity. What happened? I can't totally explain (because I'm not sure myself), but it feels like I'm crashing from the sugar high of last month. I was skip, skip, skipping along, but then I started wondering what it's all for. Am I just going to hop from factoid to factoid for the rest of my life? Sure, it can be fun, but am I going to find purpose? Or is my life's calling to be a fact looker-upper?

Everyone tells you to follow your passions, but can you make a life doing that? I don't know, since until now I've only followed my responsibilities—work, children, finding jeans that fit. Will following these curiosities lead me to something meaningful, or is this just an exercise of distraction?

So many questions. I wish I knew the answers. But until I come up with some, I'm going to keep pushing along. Onward.

Rob remarked that every business in San Antonio has either a facade shaped like the Alamo or the word "Alamo" in its title.

I checked the online Yellow Pages, and there are 1,348 Alamo entries: Alamo Gold Diamond Buyers, Alamo Classic Ponies, Alamo Stitchin Post, Alamo Bolt and Screw, Alamo City Soda Blasting, Alamo Family Foot & Ankle Care, Alamo Olive Group, Alamo City Wing Tsun, Alamo What-TheFuckDoesItHaveToDoWithYourBusiness. When there are 1,348 businesses using the word "Alamo," including it in your title would not seem to be a market differentiator, so why bother? Is it like this?

> I need to get some footwork done, but I don't
> know which doctor to go to. Oh, look! Alamo
> Family Foot & Ankle Care. That's so reassur-
> ing! I can be reminded of the slaughter while at
> the same time getting my bunions removed. I'll
> schedule with them immediately!

For any of you thinking about putting the word "Alamo" in your business title, it's a good time to remind you what the Alamo was all about.

In 1835 either Texas was fighting for its independence from Mexico or Mexico was defending its territory from rebels—depending on your perspective. In December of that year the Texans occupied a fort called the Alamo, which had originally been built as a Spanish mission. On February 23, 1836, Mexican general Santa Anna arrived at the Alamo with two thousand to three thousand troops. Over the next thirteen days the Mexicans fought against the fewer than two hundred Alamo defenders. On March 6 the Mexican troops stormed the Alamo, killing all of its defenders except some women and children.

Six weeks later, on April 21, Santa Anna fought the Texans at the Battle of San Jacinto, with the Texans rallying around the cry "Remember the Alamo!" The Texans prevailed, capturing Santa Anna.

So when you name your three-chair hair salon Alamo Hair & Nail Care, what exactly are you saying? I can cut your hair, just like Santa Anna cut the scalps of the defenders of the Alamo? Yeah, that's what you're saying, so just call it Tammy's Hair & Nail Care. No one has a problem with Tammy.

A Marshal, a Sheriff, and a Ranger Walk into a Bar

We went to dinner at our favorite Hill Country restaurant, and a group of uniformed, heavyset, older white guys sat at the table next to us. *{And no, I wasn't scared, being an older, heavyset white person myself. Besides, even I could outrun these dudes. This, folks, is the privilege I've talked about.}*

Their shirts identified them as constables, but I have no idea what those are. Marshals, sheriffs, constables, rangers—what are all those?

Marshals are part of the US Marshals Service. Okay, duh. I should have known that. USMS is the enforcement arm of the federal courts, so they protect federal judges, proceedings, and courthouses. They also chase down fugitives, arresting some 350 every day. They are responsible for transporting federal prisoners as needed. And they handle witness protection, which I'd definitely like to know more about, so we're going to have to go on a little learning diversion.

The Witness Protection Program is actually called the Witness Security Program. The program began in 1971, which surprises me because I thought it to be from the Al Capone days. Since then, 8,600 witnesses and 9,900 family members have been put in the program.

Some interesting things about witness protection:

- Participants keep their first names. That makes sense, because it would be hard to avoid responding to your real first name. But what if your first name is Lucie? One Google search and your cover would be blown.
- Participants get housed and paid a salary, but only for about six months while they look for jobs and become self-sustaining. I guess I thought these folks stayed on the payroll forever.
- If a child is being put in the witness protection program with one parent but another parent has visitation rights, then the parent not in the program has to agree to the child's participation. The other parent can keep visitation rights but has only twelve visits a year, with travel paid for by the US Marshals. Wow. I'd think the whole ex-spouse thing could cause a real problem. They're often such loudmouths.
- No one has been hurt or killed while participating in—and following the rules of—the program. Now there's

an incentive to participate. Apart from getting you killed, failing to follow the rules can get you kicked out. Best just behave.

Okay, back on the marshal, sheriff, constable, ranger highway.

A sheriff is the same concept as a marshal but on the state side. In Texas sheriffs provide security for county courts and manage the county jails. There is one sheriff for each Texas county, and these are elected positions. Sheriffs technically have jurisdiction throughout the state, but they stay out of municipalities with police departments, instead focusing on unincorporated areas. Sheriffs have deputies, and these folks are called sheriffs' deputies. See how much you're learning?

Municipalities or counties can have police officers but are not required to. Police officers only have jurisdiction within their particular municipality or county. In Texas the chief of police is a hired (not elected) position. And I think we all know what police do, generally. *{Protect, serve, and at times, assert their power excessively.}*

Constables? In Texas again—no clue what the other states do, because it's all I can do to figure out this one—there is an elected constable for each precinct within each county. They issue traffic citations, serve warrants and subpoenas, and protect the justice of the peace courts. Constables can hire deputies, and guess what they're called? Yes, constables' deputies!

Texas park rangers are part of the Texas Parks and Wildlife Department and are the law of the Texas parks system. There are also federal park rangers, of course—the law of the federal parks system.

What about Walker Texas Ranger? Was the television crime fighter a park ranger with attitude? No, he was a Texas

Ranger, an investigative law enforcement agency in Texas—like the Texas version of the FBI.

Do you want to know the favorite thing I read while learning all of this? And by favorite I mean most scary. A direct quote from the Sheriffs' Association of Texas website:

> Every Texas Sheriff, upon assuming their office, took an oath to uphold the Constitution of the United States and the Constitution of the great state of Texas. Of course, the Sheriffs of Texas are committed to uphold their oath of office. It goes without saying that Texas Sheriffs recognize that Amendment II of the Constitution provides that "the right of the people to keep and bear arms shall not be infringed" and that Amendment IV provides that "the right of the people to be secure in their persons, houses, papers, and effects, against unreasonable searches and seizures, shall not be violated."

It goes without saying? Really? Why doesn't it go without saying that, say, sheriffs recognize the right of the people to be protected from nutjobs with arsenals?

Will I Be a Leper?
I have been seeing armadillos on the property in the Hill Country. They generally run off when they see you, so they're not much of a bother. But last weekend one seemed to be stalking Rob. The armadillo came toward him, and as Rob went down the hill the armadillo walked alongside. All weekend the armadillo popped up wherever Rob was. I wondered if it might have rabies, particularly because the county recently sent a warning about rabid foxes in the area. But I

discovered that armadillos are seldom rabies carriers, so it probably just had a crush on Rob like all the gals do.

Do you know what armadillos do carry? Hansen's disease, more commonly known as leprosy. In the Southwest armadillos are naturally infected with *Mycobacterium leprae*, the bacteria that causes leprosy. The likelihood of armadillo-to-human transmission is still unknown, but I don't aim to be the one to help the scientists find out. If an armadillo doesn't run from me, I'm sure as shit running from it.

If Rob were to get leprosy, where would he even live? Are leper colonies still a thing? The only remaining US leper colony is in Kalaupapa, on the island of Molokai in Hawaii. Hawaii lifted the mandatory isolation law in 1969, effectively closing the facility, but a handful of the cured residents have chosen to remain.

I'm relieved to know that if Rob gets bitten by an infected armadillo and contracts leprosy, he won't have to move to a faraway island, as leprosy is now treatable with antibiotics.

Don't Fence Me In

In the Texas Hill Country, it's not uncommon for a line of dead coyotes to be hanging from someone's ranch fence. Why is that? Is the goal to scare away other coyotes? Is it bragging rights? What the actual fuck?

It's a little of all of that. Some folks believe hanging the dead coyotes keeps other coyotes away. Other folks say it's custom, dating back to the early 1900s when landowners paid bounties for killed coyotes and hunters hung the dead coyotes as a sort of invoice. But mainly the coyotes are hung because the landowner is bragging about his hunting skills.

So from now on, when you see coyotes hanging from a fence, think to yourself: "What a big brave man lives on that ranch. The coyotes are hung, so I guess he must be too."

Mum's the Word

I just found out that homecoming mums aren't a thing outside of Texas (except maybe in Oklahoma, but only because they like to copy us). That is shocking to me. I thought mums were standard high school practice.

What's a homecoming mum, you ask? A giant corsage, made with a chrysanthemum (now usually silk) in the center, with ribbons, pipe cleaners, cowbells, glitter paint, and other assorted tackiness attached. These things are enormous—ideally covering your entire chest and hanging down below the waist. Why so large? It's Texas, where bigger is always better.

If you have a boyfriend he will gift you your mum, and if he doesn't you will break up with him immediately and get yourself a real boyfriend. What if you don't have a boyfriend? Usually your parents will feel sorry for their lonely little precious and buy you a mum. Otherwise, you will buy one for yourself (sad) or your girlfriends will see that you're taken care of (sweet).

What will you do with the mum once you have it? You'll pin it to your chest—or rather, anchor it. You'll wear it to school all day, to the homecoming football game, then to the homecoming dance. After that you'll hang it on the wall of your bedroom, as a memento of the night you lost your virginity.

Where will you get the mum? Sometimes school groups (the cheerleaders or senior class committee, say) will sell them. If they don't, or if you want to make sure you have an extra classy mum, you'll go to a florist or crafter who specializes in making them.

How much will this mum set you back? You might be able to get a boring mum for about $50, but you should expect to pay $100 for one with any pizzazz. And if you want a mum that will really get you noticed at the homecoming game, you could pay up to $300.

What's my learning here? Apart from discovering that mums are a Texas-only phenomenon, I also learned that in the years since my high school days they have rolled out a male version of the mum, called a garter. The garter is smaller, pinned to the boy's upper arm, and a miniature version of the hideousness the girl wears.

Sometimes Texas is just fascinating. Fascinating enough for me to want to continue with Texas as my focus of learning? No, but fascinating nevertheless. I'm not yet sure what my next focus will be—hopefully something that helps me whine (and wine) less. I'm sure it's getting annoying.

!?

All the Other Places

I feel that by now I should have found some sense of purpose. Am I hoping for the impossible? Folk artist Grandma Moses didn't start painting until she was seventy-six. If she found her calling late in life, couldn't I?

Lots of older people seem happy living in retirement communities, spending their days taking photos of flowers and walking the golf course. Maybe I should be enjoying the free time and not worrying about contributing to the world in any meaningful way. Maybe I should just give up on this project, stop trying to find some greater purpose or meaning, and buy an RV.

You're probably wondering if I've seen a therapist. Yes, at Rob's urging, I went to a therapist. Not that I was opposed. I'm a long-time mental health professional groupie. When I got divorced from my first husband in 2008, I found myself in a long and dangerous depression. Mental health professionals managed to keep me alive somehow, so I figure I owe it to them to stop in and say hello on the regular. I had just gotten out of the habit, though, and my general postretirement inertia kept me from getting an appointment scheduled. I finally did, you'll be glad to know.

The therapist has encouraged me to continue with my learning project. She's noticed that while I started out almost comatose (not her exact wording, but you probably figured), Project Couch to Curiosity has made me notice things outside of myself—things that bring me joy, even. The project is lighting sparks in my brain. Devoting regular time to writing about my learnings is giving structure (albeit loose) to my days. The project is getting me comfortable with talking a bit about how I'm feeling through this transition. All of these things, the therapist likes. So I suppose I'll keep it going, if for no other reason than to please her. *{Seriously, can you imagine a worse job? She has to listen to people whine all day long. The least I could do is follow her advice every once in a while.}*

For this month I'm going to focus on other cities, states, countries, places—to step outside the small world I have created for myself.

Entreaty of Paris

A friend posted photos of her travels. I showed them to Rob in the hope that they would inspire him to say, "Hey, Lucie! Will you schedule a Paris trip for us? Let's leave Saturday." Instead the photos lead to this conversation:

"That's a cool Eiffel Tower picture," Rob said.

"Yeah. We should take one like that, shouldn't we?"

Rob looked back at his phone, done with the conversation.

"You haven't seen the Eiffel Tower, have you?" I said, hoping he'd bite this time.

"No."

"Don't you want to?"

"Yeah."

He looked back down at his phone, not taking the bait. I guess manipulation isn't always the best strategy. I'd have to be direct.

"I'd like to go to Paris. Let's schedule a trip," I said.

Rob looked up. I had his interest.

"How about next month?" I said.

Shit! As soon as "next month" escaped my lips I knew I had gone too far, too fast. I knew what would happen now. He'd startle. My impulsiveness would send him scurrying.

And sure enough. "I don't think so. I have to get back to work though," he said, and left the room.

Now I'm left to look longingly at my friend's photos, knowing it'll be a while before I can bring the idea up again. Notre Dame, lovely. Champs-Élysées, beautiful. Another Eiffel Tower pic, this one at night, stunning.

Oh, wait, that reminds me! Isn't there something about not taking Eiffel Tower pictures at night? If I can't go to Paris, at least I can learn something here.

I discovered that French copyright law protects works of art, including building design, for seventy years. Since the Eiffel Tower architects died more than seventy years ago, there's no problem with photographing the structure for commercial purposes. The lighting was designed in the 1980s, however, so it still has copyright protection. That's why you don't see nighttime photos of the tower in commercial use, stock photos, and the like.

Some European Union countries have panorama exceptions, so you can take and commercially use a photo of the whole skyline (which would include some of the copyrighted buildings), but France has no such exception.

Le plus vous en savez.

Will You Stop?

Speaking of Paris, did you know there are no stop signs in the city? There used to be one—a single one—but it up and disappeared one day. They pulled out all the stops, I suppose.

So how does traffic work with no stop signs? Chaotically, obviously, but with the understanding that the car on the right always has the right of way.

Did you know that French law requires drivers to have in their car and within reach reflective vests or jackets for each passenger, for use in case of breakdown? A safety warning triangle is also required, though it may be kept in the trunk. Oh, and all occupants of the car are required to have their passports or national ID cards on them.

I don't know why you'd ever take on driving in Paris, given how extensive the Paris Métro system is. There are more than three hundred stations, with an average distance between stations of just 548.64 meters (that's 600 yards, which I converted to meters because, you know, France). And then there are the lovely musicians, who are not ordinary buskers. Métro musicians have to audition and be selected in order to get a musician's badge.

But what's most interesting about the Métro? There is one station, Porte de Lilas, with two platforms that can be rented for use as movie sets. The station has its own set of trains that are used only for filming. The charge to use the station as a film set? About $20,000 a day.

Je voudrais to up and *aller* to Paris. The problem? *Je suis* broke.

How Do You Say?

My daughter, Mackenzie, is in Spain this semester, studying Spanish.

"I think I've got a cold," she texted.

"Oh no. Take guaifenesin/Mucinex to keep mucus loose, so it doesn't turn into a sinus infection," I replied.

"What's that sold as in Spain?"

"Sorry, sweetie, that's not in my knowledge base."

"According to the internet, Cinfatós expectorante," Mackenzie replied, after apparently looking it up.

"Glad you found it."

"I also found an American supermarket that carries the spice mix for my chili. I'm thinking about buying a few bags and just carrying them with me for the future."

"Mucinex and chili. Sounds delish."

During college I did a study abroad program in France, but that was before we could carry an instant translator and information device in our pocket. I too got sick and needed medicine, except I didn't have a cold but a yeast infection. I had to locate a pharmacy (without GPS assist) and get the attention of the pharmacist.

Excusez moi, Monsieur? I pointed to my privates and said the only relevant words I knew. *Je suis mal ici*—meaning "I am sick here." As if having the yeast infection wasn't awful enough. I damn sure wasn't going to ask if they carried Texas chili at that point.

When I told Mackenzie that story, she told me that in a pinch, garlic—vaginally inserted—cures yeast infections.

What?

Garlic does contain allicin (the liquid that makes garlic smell like garlic), which is an antifungal. But the scientific consensus is that allicin is only released if the garlic is crushed, so inserting the clove is useless and risks contaminating your hoo-ha (*le hoo-ha*) with soil bacteria.

Could you crush the garlic before inserting?

No, your vagina will rot! So just don't do that, okay?

Mark Them with Paint

I like to think I'm above a trashy headline, that I can't be sucked in. Not me—I only click on headlines about economic policy or world peace organizations.

Okay, I lied. I click on all the trash. Either trash or oddities—that's about it.

Today's newspaper oddity: In Japan police shoot paintballs at escaping cars to identify them.

The balls are called *bohan yo kara boru*—anticrime color balls—and look like baseballs the bright orange color of pylons. The balls were developed as a replacement for eggs, which toll booth attendants would throw at cars whose drivers evaded paying tolls. By the mid-1980s the use of the color balls spread to banks and retail establishments.

Convenience stores, banks, and other theft-likely businesses place the balls by the registers and in plain view. In the event of theft, the store employee can throw the ball at the perpetrator's feet. The ball bursts and splatters paint on the thief, making the outlaw easily spottable when he makes his getaway.

Are the balls effective? They're thought to have good deterrent effect, but their usage is small. The Japan National Police Agency reported in one study that the balls were used in only 3 percent of convenience store burglaries. It's just hard to think that quickly during a smash and grab, I suppose.

Now that's an article worth reading.

Christmas Chicken

While I was reading about the paint ball thing, I stumbled upon this interesting fact: In Japan, Christmas is celebrated with fried chicken. What? Christmas is celebrated? With chicken?

Japan isn't a Christian nation (instead favoring Shintoism and Buddhism), so Christmas isn't a religious holiday there. But post–World War II Japan did have an interest in all things Western, so when KFC marketed chicken as an American Christmas tradition, chicken took off. That's one theory, anyway.

Another is that the first KFC manager heard westerners asking for a turkey replacement for Christmas and thought chicken could be the thing. Yet another theory is that the manager of the first KFC in Japan (which opened in 1970), who would later become CEO, came to a Christmas party dressed as Santa. The costume played well, and he smelled a business. Still another theory: The rise of the KFC Christmas tradition came when someone ordered chicken for a party and asked for it to be delivered by Santa.

Regardless of the tradition's origins, KFC throws what financiers call a "shit-ton" of money into Christmas marketing in Japan. It's obviously working, with December 24 being KFC Japan's highest sales day of the year.

And what's KFC's highest sales day in the United States? Mother's Day.

So help me God if my kids try to take me to KFC for Mother's Day . . .

In Case of Rubber

Because I grew up speaking Spanish, and because I speak it so often here in San Antonio, Spanish phrases just pop into my mind. If someone is yammering and I wish they would shut up, I think to myself, *en boca cerrada* (in a closed mouth). The full phrase is *En boca cerrada no entran las moscas* (Flies don't get in a closed mouth), meaning you should shut your damn trap from time to time or risk a winged insect laying its larvae in your mouth.

I recently thought of the Spanish phrase *por si las de hule*, which means something like "on the chance that" or "just in case." *Hule* means rubber, I know, so "in chance of rubber"? Where does that phrase come from?

I put my sister Edith on the case. She's planning to move to Mexico soon, so she needs to learn all of the Spanish phrases. She reported that the phrase comes from bullfighting. The floor of the bullring infirmary was protected with rubber, so the phrase basically means "protection in the event of a bloodbath."

¡Que interesante!

The Golden Hydrant

Rob and I are planning to visit San Francisco. I could use a little adventure.

On Rob's list of things to see is the golden fire hydrant. Fisherman's Wharf or Coit Tower, sure, but the golden hydrant? What's that about?

On April 18, 1906, at 5:12 a.m., San Francisco was hit with a 7.9 magnitude earthquake. The quake lasted less than a minute, but the tremors ruptured gas lines, causing fires to break out throughout the city. The quake also ruptured water mains and left streets impassable, making it impossible for firefighters to combat the blaze. More than 90 percent of the city was consumed by fire.

As fire approached the Mission District, residents began looking for functioning water hydrants. They discovered one on Church Street. The horses pulling the fire engines were too exhausted to climb, but residents helped firefighters pull the engines up the hill to the hydrant. The district was saved.

Sadly, much of the rest of the city was not. The fires continued for four days. Ultimately more than three thousand people perished. Two-thirds of the city's population of four hundred thousand was left homeless. More than twenty-eight thousand buildings were destroyed.

In the 1960s, as a commemoration of this fight to save the Mission District, the hydrant was painted gold. Now local residents and firefighters gather annually on April 18 at 5:12 a.m. to celebrate, applying a fresh coat of gold paint to the hydrant.

Pay it a visit on your next trip to San Francisco. It's on Twentieth and Church Streets, right at Dolores Park.

A Little Shampoo

When Rob and I were in San Francisco, we stayed at a hotel with wall dispensers for the shampoo and conditioner. I can't figure out whether I love that (save the planet!) or hate that (conditioner looks kinda like . . .).

I would think hotels are happy to make this change though—to avoid spending money on individual bottles of beauty while also getting tagged as environmentally responsible.

Of course, switching to bulk-size product is the right thing to do since it reduces waste, both of the bottles themselves and of their contents. Though some hotels donate partially used toiletries, most throw away all bottles with a broken seal, even if there is product remaining inside. *{So don't feel guilty about taking those half-used bottles home with you, folks! In fact, hotels are even okay with you taking unused bottles with you. They hope you'll lather up at home and have fond memories of your hotel stay. While you're pilfering things, swipe the slippers, which hotels are going to trash anyway. And five-finger the branded notepad and pen, which hotels provide to their guests as part of their marketing efforts. Just don't take the towels, bathrobes, iron, hairdryer, pillows, bedding, radio, remote control, lightbulbs, or paintings. (Really, folks, I shouldn't have to tell you this, but I guess all your mothers didn't raise you right.) And whatever you do, don't* *take the Bible—unless you're going to hell anyway, I suppose, in which case it's tacky but not the cause of your eternal damnation.}*

And now I'm wondering why most hotels make you call down for toothpaste instead of providing it with the other toiletries. The answer is because hotel grading companies (like AAA) don't grade hotels on toothpaste, since so few have it. But, duh, the hotels don't have it because they're not graded on it, so that seems circular.

Of course if hotels did provide toothpaste, I definitely wouldn't want them to stray from single-use containers on those. Can you imagine if you went to a hotel with bulk toothpaste in the bathroom? That shit's damn sure not going in my mouth.

While in San Francisco, Rob and I had a chance to do more talking.

"I need to figure out what's going to make me happy. I'm still a bit lost."

"Yeah."

"Maybe I should just go back to work."

"Do you really want to?"

"I don't know what I want. I could do part-time contract work, I suppose."

"You'd just end up working full time."

He's right, I would. Part-time work, for me, always ends up being full-time work for part-time pay. I tried that after I had my second kid. I was supposed to have an 80 percent schedule, but really I just had 80 percent pay with the same damn schedule. It wasn't the law firm's fault but mine. I just couldn't make myself walk out the door when there was work to do. But if I were doing contract work, I would be getting paid if I worked more, so maybe that is the answer.

Maybe.

Call to Prayer

My daughter, Mackenzie, who is still in Spain for the semester, visited Tunisia. We talked on the phone, and she mentioned that she hadn't gotten much sleep there because she was awakened every morning at 5:39 a.m. by the call to prayer. The call to prayer is delivered from the local mosque five times a day, reminding Muslims to come to mandatory prayer.

I knew there were many calls to prayer throughout the day, but I didn't realize just how early the first one is. Turns out there are five Salah or Salat (prayer) times: Fajr (dawn), Dhuhr (after midday), Asr (afternoon), Maghrib (after sunset), and Isha (night). The exact times vary by location and time of year, because they're based on the sun. In Tunisia right now, they're at approximately 6 a.m., 12:10 p.m., 2:45 p.m., 5 p.m., and 6:20 p.m. *{I can't even get myself to church on Christmas and Easter. Not that I even intend to anymore. These days, I limit my churchgoing to weddings and funerals, and those seldom happen five times a day.}*

Women and men both pray five times a day, though women are exempt during Shark Week and after childbirth. They pray in a slightly different position, for modesty reasons. For example, they do not take their arms out of their shawls/sleeves as men would because that would expose their forearms. If women and men are congregated praying, the women stand behind the men. Women generally pray silently rather than aloud (though if they are praying alone, they must vocalize just enough so they can hear themselves). There are other requirements, but suffice it to say there are some gender differences.

Better than that learning is the reason Mackenzie was in Tunisia: my grandfather is buried there, or actually *not* buried there because they never found his body. During

World War II, the plane he was piloting was shot down by the Germans in the Tyrrhenian Sea, off the coast of Sicily. Rescue flights were unable to locate him or any of the other men shot down.

My grandfather is memorialized at the North Africa American Cemetery in Tunis, in the Tablets of the Missing. Because Mackenzie is in Spain, which is reasonably close to Tunisia, she decided to visit his memorial.

How kind of a human is Mackenzie? She took photos of the cemetery, the tablets, and my grandfather's name on the wall and forwarded them to my mother. She then got my mother on FaceTime and walked her around the cemetery. Mama, who thought she would never have a chance to see her father's memorial, bawled.

When a daughter thinks of doing something so very meaningful for her grandmother? Well, it makes a mama proud. {*And a little ashamed, to be honest. I was in school in Europe for a year, and it never occurred to me to go over to Tunisia. But it did occur to me to go to Oktoberfest!*}

State Stupid

I am unable to locate US states on a map. In college a friend gave me a puzzle—with wooden pieces in the shapes of the states—designed to help three-year-olds learn their state placements. I played and played it until I knew all of the states cold. But it has been some years, and the locations are long forgotten. {*This reminder might be helpful: I lived in Mexico during elementary school. While all of you were busy learning the states and capitals, I was playing soccer (fútbol, actually). Not that I learned soccer either.*}

I decided it was time to use an online quiz to relearn the state locations. It took me twenty tries to get 100 percent. My sad scores were 40, 49, 64, 60, 60, 74, 77, 69, 81, 89, 93, 81, 85, 82, 91, 85, 91, 91, 85, 100.

Rob walked in while I was doing this. "I still don't understand how you don't know where the states are," he said.

"I think it's because my brain is full up with more critical information, like my kids' birthdates, the dog's vaccination schedule, and Britney Spears's conservatorship status."

"Of course it is," Rob said. "May I take the test? I'm curious how I'd do."

He got 100 percent on his one and only try.

After this humiliating exercise I decided there must be tricks for remembering the location of these states—and there are. I'll share these with you, not because I think you have this knowledge gap (of course you know your states). But maybe there's a toddler in your life who hasn't yet been schooled?

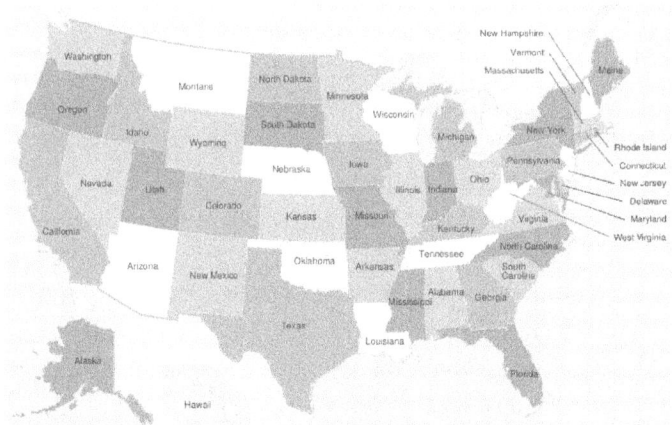

- The three leftmost states on the map, bottom to top, spell COW: California, Oregon, Washington.
- The state up top that looks like a face is <u>Montana</u>, because it looks like a man.

- The unmemorable square below Montana is <u>Wy</u>oming, which you will remember because: <u>Why</u> is this one so forgettable?
- The two below it? UC (you'll remember these, you'll see—which sounds like UC): Utah and Colorado.
- Going down from California, bordering Mexico, is CANT—as in, you <u>can't</u> cross the border—California, Arizona, New Mexico, Texas.
- The five states stacked on top of Texas all have Ks in them: O<u>k</u>lahoma, <u>K</u>ansas, Nebras<u>k</u>a, South Da<u>k</u>ota, and North Da<u>k</u>ota.
- The next pancake stack, to the right of Texas, spells MIMAL: Minnesota, Iowa, Missouri, Arkansas, and Louisiana.
- Going from Iowa, your I's are next to each other on your face, so next to Iowa is Illinois. But you're weird, so you have three eyes! There's Indiana!
- Right below that is Kentucky, because it looks like a fried chicken drumstick.
- The one up top that looks like a mitten? It starts with <u>mi</u> like mitten—Michigan.
- On the right side of the map, Maine is the main state—because it's at the top right.
- Of the two states to the left of Maine, Vermont is the one shaped like a V. I'll be damned if I know what the other one is. You're on your own there. *{Just kidding, I looked it up for you. It's New Hampshire, which is absolutely not memorable, so that one isn't my fault.}*
- I have no trouble getting New York (the biggest one up there) or Rhode Island (the smallest one), but the one in the middle? It's Connecticut, because it connects Rhode Island to New York.

Okay, you're ready for a map quiz now. Get your husband in the room and dazzle him with your genius.

Día de los Muertos

I am going to San Miguel de Allende for the Day of the Dead celebrations. Having lived in Mexico as a kid, I know there are two different days celebrated on November 1 and 2, but I don't quite remember what's what about them. Both days together are called Día de los Muertos, or Day of the Dead.

November 1 is Día de los Angelitos, or Day of the Little Angels. Because children are without sin in Catholic tradition (unless they're real assholes, but even then they know not what they do), those who die shoot straight up to heaven as *angelitos*. On November 1 their spirits are said to come down for a quick visit. Families make altars decorated with toys and bright marigolds to guide the spirits to them.

November 2 is Día de los Difuntos, or Day of the Deceased. This is the day deceased adults are celebrated. Again, families make altars to attract their loved ones, but since they're luring adult spirits they fill the altars with food and booze. Families also gather at the cemeteries, celebrating their loved ones with music and decorated gravesites.

All in all, the celebration is lovely. Rather than being a time of sadness, it's a time of family, food, drink, parades, color, and joy.

One interesting tradition of Día de los Muertos is the Catrinas, skeleton figures celebrating the dead. For San Miguel de Allende's Día de los Muertos celebration, people dress up like Catrinas. Face painters fill the streets, painting people's faces with bright colors. Flower vendors line the square, selling elaborate floral headpieces. And at night all of the Catrinas dance in the streets.

Where did Catrinas come from? The Catrina derived from a skeleton (*calavera*, in Spanish) figure drawn by José Guadalupe Posada. The image was of a woman skeleton dressed in a fancy hat. Posada titled the piece *La Calavera Garbancera* and intended it as satire of women who were common mestizos (mixed-race Spanish and indigenous people, who often sold garbanzo beans in the streets and were thus called *garbanceras*) but pretended to be European aristocrats. His point was that these wannabe-fancy folks were pretty on the outside but dead on the inside.

CALAVERA CATRINA

Muralist Diego Rivera, inspired by Posada, included the image in one of his murals. He called the woman La Catrina (borrowing from the word *catrín*, which was a sort of dandy).

Isn't that just dandy?

More Mexico
Speaking of Mexico, I've heard that Mexico City is sinking, but is that true?

Sadly, it is. Mexico City (then called Tenochtitlán) was built in 1325 by the Aztecs in a mountainous valley, on what was essentially an island surrounded by lakes.

When the Spaniards conquered the city in the early 1500s, they expanded the city by draining the lakes and building on them. They bored wells into the aquifer, for use as the city's water source. As the water was removed from the aquifer, the soil compressed. As the city grew, it expanded on this uneven soil. Water needs increased, causing more drainage from the aquifer and making the ground more unstable.

To make matters worse, because buildings and roads were constructed with concrete and asphalt, rainwater was trapped in the city, unable to seep through the ground to replenish the aquifer.

The city continues to extract more water than is naturally replenished, and the ground continues to compress. Some areas are sinking at a rate of more than three feet a year. Climate change has only worsened the problem.

The sinking has caused structural damage to buildings, making many look all catawampus (which I still say should always be spelled "cattywampus"). In 1989 Mexico City's lopsided Metropolitan Cathedral finally cracked down the middle and had to be supported with reinforcing scaffolding until it could be restored. Underground pipes have been crushed throughout the city, causing significant disruptions to the water supply.

The subsidence cannot be undone, and further subsidence is inevitable. Scientists predict that the city will continue to compress, with full compression reached in about 150 years. Water supply disruptions will continue, and water contamination is likely. Alternative sources of drinking water will be critical.

Well, that sinks.

The Year of the Lord

"Would non-Christian countries say it's 2019?" Rob said.

"What?" I said.

"Do non-Christian countries use the same BC/AD year numbering system we do?"

"I don't know, but that's interesting. You should look it up."

"But what's the point of you writing about all of that stuff if you won't look things up for me?"

Ah, I'd forgotten. Rob had months earlier asked me to look up "small beer" and "almoner." But I pushed back a little, just for fun.

"So, wait, so from your perspective, the point of the book I'm writing is so I can be your information concierge?"

"Exactly."

You would think I would let it go at that and leave him to look the question up himself. But here's where he's sneaky. He knows he has planted the seed and I won't be able to help myself. I will look it up. And then I won't even be coy about it. I'll have to tell him what I found. So here we go.

The United States and most other countries use the Gregorian calendar, which marks years from the supposed date of Christ's birth (supposed, because when he was born is disputed).

The countries that do not use the Gregorian calendar are Afghanistan and Iran (which use the Solar Hijri calendar), Ethiopia (which uses the Ethiopian calendar), and Nepal (which uses the Bikram Sambat calendar).

So what year is it in these countries right now (that is, in October 2019)?

- Afghanistan and Iran: 1398 (with year one being based on prophet Mohammed's migration to Medina in 622 BC)

- Ethiopia: 2012 (with year one being 7 BC, the year in which they believe Christ was born)
- Nepal: 2076 (for the life of me, I can't find anything that tells me what year one is; I give up)

I reported my findings to Rob, just as he knew I would.

"Thanks for looking that up. And what calendars preceded the Gregorian?" he said.

"The Julian. The Gregorian is a correction to the Julian. Something to do with leap year. I don't exactly remember."

"Will you look into that?"

"Nope."

"Why?"

"Because I don't really care."

"I care."

"Then you should definitely look into that."

"Well, if you're going to be a quitter."

That's me! Lucie, the historical calendar quitter.

And on that note, I close out my month of learning about other places. How am I feeling? Honestly, not great. WTF is wrong with me?

!?
All the Soul

I've spent several days churning over my funk. As I've thought (okay, obsessed) about it, I have come to see that the problem is that I'm not doing what I set out to do in retirement. Remember how my plan was to do good in this world? Well, I've done none, and I feel selfish and rudderless.

I suppose now is the time to tell you about that first month postretirement, the month before I kicked off Project Couch to Curiosity. Yes, I should have told you about it before, but I barely knew you then.

I have mentioned that as I drove to work in the mornings, I listened to NPR stories about the immigrant crisis. I was disturbed (as we all were) about how immigrants were being incarcerated, about how children were being separated from their parents, about how our country could treat desperate people so horribly. South-central Texas, where I live, was an epicenter of the crisis. The US-Mexico border is three hours away, and one of the larger immigrant detention centers was just two hours down the road. The Refugee and Immigrant Center for Education and Legal Services (RAICES), based in

San Antonio, was one of the key groups trying to help immigrants. Basically, the crisis was unfolding in my backyard.

While I was still working, I went to an information session about volunteering with RAICES, which was training lawyers to help migrants with the asylum process. I was a Spanish-speaking lawyer, and I knew I could help. The time commitment was more than I could manage while working, but knowing I was needed at the detention centers made me all the more eager to quit my job.

Not long after the cringy resignation text I sent to my boss, I found myself in Dilley, Texas, where mothers and their children were held together, but often in different parts of the facility. I met with migrants (mostly from Guatemala, El Salvador, and Honduras) and asked them to tell me their stories so I could help present them to the immigration judge. I write that sentence matter-of-factly, because I don't have the words to explain what it's like to ask a mother—a mother who has been through things so horrible that her only choice was to grab her children and run, a mother who walked more than fifteen hundred miles with her children on her hip, a mother whose children were pulled away from her just as she got to "safety," a mother who has been sleeping in a series of cold jail cells for two weeks, desperate for her children—to trust me, a stranger.

And how could I, a woman who just quit her job by drunken text, possibly process those stories entrusted to me? I simply couldn't. I was on unsteady emotional ground. When I got home from a day at the detention center, I wept. I trembled as I drove to the center the next day. I started having intrusive thoughts, ones I knew signaled the start of a depressive spiral.

I did not have the strength to help these women.

So I quit going down to Dilley. I left those families in those cages, and I sat on my couch watching *90 Day Fiancé*, and the shame of that made me unable to do a single thing other than queue up another episode.

Yes, the "chase each curiosity" project got me off the couch, but now the project feels petty, meaningless, and indulgent. And now that I've told you all of this, I just want to go to sleep.

I've decided to spend my month focusing on spirituality, religion, and soul stuff. Maybe I'll stumble across something that will be meaningful to me. Do I expect to find the Lord? Doubtful, unless he peek-a-boos me right now! *{He didn't.}*

One warning: Retirement has freed me to be more open about my religious beliefs—or more accurately, lack thereof. If you have strong feelings about religion, feel free to turn to the next chapter. I promise it won't hurt my feelings.

Why wasn't I able to speak freely about my nonreligion when employed? Because being a good attorney is important, but being good at getting business is even more important. When you first start working at a law firm, that part is a surprise. You went to law school because you were inspired by *To Kill a Mockingbird* or *12 Angry Men*. *{Truly, those are the only two inspirations. Ask any lawyer you know. Well, any lawyer over forty-five anyway. The younger generation might have been inspired by* Clueless.*}* Then you find out your job is more *Death of a Salesman*.

I worked for a law firm for almost seventeen years. Because so many folks in this part of the country are conservative Christians, it hardly made good sense to declare myself as "other."

After the law firm, I went to work for a tractor dealership—also a very Jesus-y demographic. I worked with the human resources team, so it was zero percent advisable for me to talk about religion.

Besides, I wasn't really sure how I felt about religion. I tried to believe. I really did. But after years of making myself go to church and finding myself interested only in the stained-glass windows, the choir, and the hour of my escape, I acknowledged it wasn't going to take.

Of course, I'm bound by values like mutual respect and compassion. And I feel more gratefulness, connectedness, and peace than I did in my younger years. But religion? Not so much.

I respect any religious faith you have. I don't reject another's faith (unless it's an assholey faith, then I absolutely reject that). I just don't have much of it myself.

Anyhow, I'm ready to dive into all my curiosities of the soul. Off to learn.

Move Those Eyes

I confessed to my psychiatrist how I am feeling, and how I'm finding myself drinking wine to cope with those feelings.

When I thought about retirement, I didn't imagine that I would so often have a glass of wine in hand. You'd think if I were going to have a substance abuse problem, it would have manifested by now. But here I am, retired and drinking more than I know is advisable.

Maybe work provided some protection for me, like bowling bumpers. It kept me busy late into the day, so I had less time to drink in the evenings. I knew I'd have to wake up early and be mentally alert when I got to work, so I had to be more cautious about how much I drank. Work kept me from falling into the gutter.

In retirement, my life is unstructured. I don't allow myself to drink until 5 or 6 p.m., but that's earlier than I ever started drinking when working. I don't have to go to sleep at any particular time, so sure, I'll have another glass or three. Do I need to be snappy tomorrow? Not at all, so make it four.

I've always been an addict—studying, smoking, reading, working, eating, exercising, shopping, -ing, -ing, -ing. Some of my addictions have been healthy (exercising) or societally rewarded (studying, working). Some have been societally encouraged (shopping), and some have been victimless crimes (reading). Many have been dangerous (smoking, eating), but only to me, so tolerated. But there have always been addictions.

I've always stayed away from hard drugs, knowing my propensities. *{Who among you (even those of you who haven't met me in person) doubts that I would adore cocaine?}* In retrospect, I should have been more cautious about alcohol too. I come from a long line of alcoholics, so why wouldn't wine be equally risky to me?

The psychiatrist suggested I try a new (for me) form of psychotherapy—Eye Movement Desensitization and Reprocessing (EMDR), a therapy directed at healing trauma. The process is weird and goes something like this: *{I say "something like this" because I'm no doctor, so don't rely on me for real medical knowledge. Like every other damn thing that comes out of my mouth, this is a vague picture of things, which may or may not be accurate.}*

First you vomit a list of all traumas you've experienced in your life—just a list of the issues you know you need to work through. The vomit session is not fun. You and the therapist agree on the order you will address them in.

The therapist asks you to identify one particular part of a trauma that you remember. You focus on that single issue or memory. The therapist moves her finger back and forth (left, right, left, right), and as you think of that memory, you track her finger—like a hypnosis watch, but it's her finger. *{You can instead hold buzzers in your hands that buzz left-right-left-right, which is what I did, because if I had been shaking my head back and forth I would have vomited for real.}*

She pauses and asks you what you're feeling at that moment. She asks you to hold the thought in your mind, and again you track her finger back and forth. You keep doing that, over and over—stop tracking, what are you thinking now, hold that thought in your head, track the finger again, stop tracking, and on and on and on until you've said everything you have to say about the issue, and the emotional pain of the trauma somehow dissipates. The therapist has you say a positive statement of how you'd like to feel about that event (e.g., "I am strong") and "installs" that statement in your brain through more of the back and forth. As you do this, you talk your own way through the trauma.

Let's say you were traumatized because you saw your dog get hit by a car. You may start with the memory of the car, move to berating yourself for letting your dog off leash, and wind your way through all of your feelings until you come to the acceptance that it was an accident that could have happened to anyone.

While there have been studies showing EMDR to be effective, there has been no conclusion about how EMDR works. A primary theory is that the back-and-forth eye motion simulates REM, a sleep stage during which you use both hemispheres of your brain to process and consolidate information, with the right hemisphere processing your emotions and the left making meaning of them. EMDR is thought to use the brain's natural healing process to make sense of the trauma, making it less triggering.

We'll see how EMDR ends up working for me. So far it's forcing me to talk about things I haven't discussed before. It's allowing me to examine every aspect of why and how I responded to certain situations. Then it's getting me to process my feelings about it. So yeah, this is good soul work, and I'm happy I'm doing it. {Oh, and no, I'm not going to talk about *what the traumas are. That's for a whole other book—one that I have zero desire to write, thank you.}*

Bless You

Somewhere along the line I stopped blessing people when they sneeze. The whole ritual just seems odd to me. We don't bless people when they cough, so why would we when they sneeze? Do we really need to call for God's help over nasal discharge? Isn't he more needed elsewhere?

Rob thinks my refusal to participate in this social convention is a bit rude—or silly, anyway—but he is willing to overlook my rudeness, because what choice does he have? But since I know he prefers some sort of blessing after the sneeze, at times I just say *Salud*—meaning health, and being the typical blessing for sneezing in Latin America. Saying it acknowledges the social norm but doesn't pull God away from his otherwise busy day.

A friend explained that your heart stops when you sneeze, thus the need for heavenly assistance. I had heard that before, but really?

No, not really. Or maybe a little bit. Here's how it works. Your nose gets irritated, you suck in a deep breath, you tighten your chest muscles, and then you achoo the irritant out. During this process the pressure in your chest changes, and your heart rhythm quickly adjusts to the changes. But no, it doesn't stop, so you don't need a God-defibrillator.

So I'll keep with the *Salud* to make nice, but I still refuse to bother the Big Man.

Ain't Got Much Religion

When I was a young adult, I made an effort to believe what they were teaching us at Sunday school and church. I found the lessons interesting culturally (Christianity is everywhere, so it's good to know something about it), but I thought something was wrong with me because I was unable to internalize them. The stories always read as myths to me. Perseus saved Andromeda from the sea monster? That's cool! They rolled back the rock, and Jesus was gone? Great story!

I once heard an analogy about religion. You can stand in a garage for as long as you want, but it's never going to make you a car. That's how I feel in church. I can go as many times as you'd like, but I'm never going to turn into a proper Christian.

Ricky Gervais makes an argument I like. There are three thousand gods across the religions. Christians believe in only one of those gods, rejecting the other 2,999. Agnostic atheists (as he calls himself) believe in just one fewer god than Christians. Everyone is a nonbeliever as to all gods but their own, so being a nonbeliever of someone's one god shouldn't be that controversial.

All of this gets me to what I want to learn. What percentage of the US population identifies as nonbelievers?

The Religious Landscape study released by Pew Research in 2014 says this:

- 70.6 percent. Christian
- 5.9 percent. Non-Christian faiths (Jewish, Buddhist, etc.)
- 22.8 percent. Unaffiliated or religious "nones" (atheists, agnostics, nothing in particular)

The trend is moving away from religion and toward religious nothingness. A more recent Pew study, a smaller telephone study done in 2019, showed 65 percent identifying as Christian and 26 percent identifying as "nones." Maybe I'm not so alone in my irreligion as I feel.

All the Soul

185

Of course, in Texas we're driving the national averages up. Pew says 77 percent of Texans are Christian, and the other 23 percent lie and say they are. *{Just kidding. Pew doesn't call out the liars. But they should!}*

So yeah, I'm still fairly alone down here. But if I live long enough, I may not always be.

The Power of Prayer

A friend was telling me about someone who was healed by prayer. When I rolled my eyes, she said, "You know, I believe that prayer really can heal." She went on to explain that there are scientific studies proving this. She said there are even studies proving that retroactive healing works—that is, that you can pray today for someone to be healed in the past.

I asked her how retroactive healing works. She said something about parallel universes and time not being on a continuum and, well, I have no idea what she said because my brain checked out, but I did listen enough to know I wanted to look this shit up.

Let me say first that I do believe love and good vibes heal. I believe we can support people, and this can promote their healing. I believe a positive attitude can help the process. I believe we can pray for comfort and peace, and this can reduce pain and help give us strength in our healing process. But do I believe I can cure a kid's cancer by praying hard enough? No, I do not. And I certainly don't believe I can pray now for a kid who had cancer in 1990 to be healed, and that his 1990 prospects will be made better by my effort.

On to what I found out. Some studies show that intercessory prayer (prayers on another's behalf) may be helpful, but others show that it's not, and some show that it's harmful. Praying on someone's behalf isn't a scientifically proven treatment plan.

How the Hell Did I Not Know That?

186

And the retrospective prayer stuff? A study by Leonard Leibovici looked at people who had bloodstream infections between 1990 and 1996. In 2000 these prior patients were divided into a control group and a prayer group, and the prayer group was prayed over. When Leibovici looked back at their hospital stays from the 1990s, the group that was prayed over (reminder: in 2000) had shorter hospital stays and fewer days of fever (reminder: in the 1990s). While Leibovici did report these findings, he published them as a joke. His point was that it makes no sense to study prayer in a randomized, controlled study.

I'm not saying you shouldn't pray because its benefits aren't scientifically provable. That's the whole thing with religion—it's based on faith, not science. So pray away, if that's your fancy! Just don't be pissed that I don't join the prayer chain.

So am I saying higher powers are bullshit? No, I don't think that either. There are so many things in this world I don't understand.

Why do humans have a conscience? Why do we feel pain and sorrow? Why do we feel guilty when we don't do the dishes before bed? Perhaps these were all evolutionarily beneficial traits, or perhaps they weren't. I don't know, and I'm curious.

Why is there a sun, planets, chocolate? I don't know the source of their power, but I know there's something big there, and I'm curious.

Why do we have intuition? Is that some version of the Holy Spirit, or is something else at play? Intuition is powerful, and I'm curious.

I am recommitting to remember that there are big things in this world I don't understand. Rather than accept or reject every thought, belief, or theory, it's okay to do nothing, to wait, and to learn.

Hanukkah, oh Hanukkah

It's November, so Hanukkah is coming soon. For my non-Jewish friends, you might need a refresher on what this holiday is all about.

Hanukkah—the Festival of Lights—celebrates the rededication of the second temple in Jerusalem, after the Maccabean Revolt. What's that, you ask? Well, I figured I'd look that up for you. And because I wanted to keep it simple, I looked in KidzSearch, the Encyclopedia for Kids. It says this:

> The Maccabean Revolt was an insurrection
> by Jewish patriots (the Maccabees) against
> the Seleucid Empire and parties who wished
> to adopt Greek culture. The Seleucid Empire,
> which controlled present-day Syria and
> Israel, sought to make the Jewish people more
> Greek-like. The Seleucid Emperor Antiochus
> IV Epiphanes installed a Greek idol Zeus in
> Jerusalem's Temple and forbade Jewish prac-
> tices. Jewish individuals who wished to keep
> their identity and traditions did not like what
> Seleucids were doing and decided to fight
> against them. Judah Maccabee and his brothers
> led the rebellion, liberated Jerusalem, and
> restored the Temple. The Maccabees won the
> war and reestablished the kingdom of Judah.

I don't know about your kids, but seriously? This is an encyclopedia for kids? "The Seleucid Emperor Antiochus IV Epiphanes," for *kids*?

Here's a simpler explanation of the story. Well, not the whole story, but the key parts.

In about 170 BC a king in Israel named Antiochus wanted everyone to worship the Greek gods. He banned Judaism, trashed the Jewish temple, and filled it with statues of Greek gods.

A group of folks called the Maccabees decided to fight against Antiochus. They were a small group but managed to defeat the king. They cleaned up the temple and restarted its rituals, including keeping the menorah (which symbolized knowledge and creation) lit through the night. They made a new menorah but were only able to find a small jar of oil to light the candles. There was only enough for one day, and it would take eight days to get more. But they lit the candles, and miraculously the candles stayed lit for eight days.

The Maccabees held a celebration to rededicate the temple. Hanukkah ("inauguration" in Hebrew) commemorates this dedication with a celebration lasting eight days.

Yes, Jewish friends, I know there's a lot more to it. Sorry, I did my best.

And Now Passover
Speaking of Jewish holidays, my daughter, Mackenzie, mentioned the orange on the seder plate. "Huh? What orange on the seder plate?" I asked.

She explained that the orange is a modern addition. *{The traditional items on the plate are zeroah (a shankbone, representing the sacrificial lamb), beitzah (a roasted egg, representing springtime and renewal), maror and chazeret (bitter herbs, often horseradish, representing the bitterness of slavery), charoset (a sweet fruit paste or salad, representing the mortar used by the Jews to build the Egyptian pharaohs' buildings), and karpas (greens, often parsley, representing spring).}*

The orange is intended to symbolize solidarity with the queer community. You are to take a slice and eat it, then spit out the seeds as a rejection of homophobia.

"Orange you smart for knowing that," I said.

"I'm going upstairs now," she said.

Now Do Ramadan

Since I am learning about Hanukkah and Passover, it seems a good time to refresh my recollection about Ramadan. Here's about all I know: It's a month (but I don't know which one) during which Muslims pray and fast. That's the total of my knowledge.

When is Ramadan? The ninth month of the Islamic calendar.

How many months does the Islamic calendar have? Twelve. It is a lunar calendar, with the new moon marking the first day of each month. Each month is twenty-nine or thirty days long, depending on moon cycles. Thus a full year is 354 or 355 days. Because the Islamic calendar runs ten to eleven days behind our Gregorian calendar, the dates of the ninth month vary from year to year.

During Ramadan, Muslims fast from dawn to sunset, abstaining from food, drink (including water!), cigarettes, and sex, as a devotion to God. After sunset, mosques and soup kitchens provide meals, feasts really, to end the day of fasting. Fancy hotels also make a thing of it, providing large buffets for their guests and often serving a predawn breakfast to those about to begin their fast.

What if you're sick? Still no water? Those who are mentally or physically ill are exempt from the fasting requirement. Also exempt are prepubescent children, the elderly, people who are traveling, and women who are breastfeeding, pregnant, or menstruating.

If you miss a fasting day—because you are traveling, for example—you may make it up later during the year. If you are unable to make up the lost fasting day—because you are ill or elderly, say—you are expected to provide a meal to the needy for each day missed. If you choose not to fast for no good reason, your children are expected to make up your missed fasting days upon your death.

What if you live where the sun doesn't rise or set—like Alaska? You follow the sunrise-sunset schedule of another city, such as Mecca.

The end of Ramadan is marked by a three-day celebration, Eid al-Fitr, where people gather, eat, exchange gifts, and celebrate.

Note to self: Schedule all gatherings during Ramadan after sunset so your Muslim friends can fully participate.

Zen Koan

If there's anything to be known about religion or spirituality, I don't know it. Don't pick me for your Trivial Pursuit team if those categories are in the box. Those, and history. And sports. And science. Oh shit, I guess I'm the worst team member all around. Except entertainment! I can kick ass at entertainment questions. Unless they're about directors. I don't know anything about directors.

To prove my lack of knowledge, I am going to confess that I have no idea what a Zen koan is. The phrase was mentioned in a story I read, and nothing came to mind. Blank slate.

Trusty Merriam-Webster tells me a koan is "a paradox to be meditated upon that is used to train Zen Buddhist monks to abandon ultimate dependence on reason and to force them into gaining sudden intuitive enlightenment."

The only koan I'd really heard of is the question, What is the sound of one hand clapping? Another well-known koan is:

Q. What is Buddha?
A. Three pounds of flax.

And hell if I know what that means, so now I have to go down that rabbit hole.

Apparently robes are made from three pounds of flax. Buddha is in his robe. But anyone can wear a robe, so we are all Buddha.

That's interesting. But let me get this straight. If I throw on a Snuggie and leather sandals, I can get instant enlightenment?

Pray Tell

I was listening to the podcast *On Being*. Host Krista Tippett was interviewing science reporter Erik Vance, who explained that the brain's purpose is to make predictions based on your experiences. You learn when you do *x*, *y* happens, and in the future when you are presented with *x*, the brain responds based on this prior experience. Vance said the brain is so good at making these predictions that it can often adjust on the expectation of your doing *x*.

He explained that with medicine, for example, your brain anticipates that you will get better when you take a pill. It will make the adjustment and you'll get better, even if the pill is a placebo. The "theater of medicine" is critical to your brain's response. Getting handed a pill by someone in a white lab coat helps your brain predict and respond in a way it wouldn't if a pill were handed to you by a guy in cutoffs in a garage.

Vance said some diseases don't have a strong placebo response. Placebo doesn't help with Alzheimer's or cancer, for example, but it can help with depression, pain, Parkinson's, and a host of other conditions.

He suggested that alternative therapies can be important to your brain's prediction response. If you're a lapsed Catholic, you should go to church. If you believe drinking fizzy drinks helps soothe your stomach, you should drink fizzy drinks. You should do whatever you think might help, in the hope your brain will agree with you and make adjustments to make you better.

Vance believes that skeptics aren't doing themselves any favors. You should want your brain to believe in healing, so your brain will heal. It's your superpower.

This is a good reminder for me to stop being judgmental about the power of prayer. I must quit acting like I know everything about everything, because even scientists acknowledge they know almost nothing about everything. As Einstein put it, "The more I learn, the more I realize how much I don't know."

Gideon Up

Bibles. How do they get in hotel rooms? Are they donated by Gideon? Or churches? Or by Jesus himself?

Let's start with the story of Gideon. And since I'm not a religious scholar (or even a dilettante), this could be all wrong. Don't go running your mouth off at church with this story and have people think you a heathen. Just tuck it in the back of your brain as "maybe just somewhat right."

The Israelites started worshipping false idols, which pissed God off. So God sicced the Midianites (a nomadic tribe) on the Israelites and for seven long years let the Midianites steal the Israelites' crops.

For reasons I don't know, God finally decided he was cool with the Israelites. He came to Gideon, an Israelite, and told

Gideon he could overthrow the Midianites. Gideon didn't believe it was really God, so he asked him to prove it. God did a few miracles and alas, Gideon was a believer.

Gideon then got a group of people to fight the Midianites. God thought the group was too big and wanted Gideon to face an unfair fight. *{God sounds like a bit of an asshole here, just sayin'.}* So God had Gideon tell the army folks they could leave if they were afraid. Lots left. God still thought the group was too big, so he told Gideon to lead the troops to the water and dismiss anyone who drank like a dog. Lots of dog-drinkers, apparently, because Gideon was left with three hundred men.

Gideon knew he was screwed with such a small number, but God said, "Gideon, we got this!"

God had the Midianites dream that they were getting rolled over by a piece of bread, which somehow made them think they were going to get crushed by the Israelites. Then God sent Gideon and the Israelites over to the Midianites with trumpets and jars. The Israelites blew the trumpets and smashed the jars on the ground. The Midianites, already fearful that they were going to be crushed, panicked and ran away.

And Israel was saved thanks to God (who put Israel in the mess in the first place, but whatever).

Why the long story? Context, my friends.

Now the story of how Gideons International came about. In 1898 two businessmen were staying at a hotel and realized they were both Christians. They decided they should bring the Word to the heathens. They prayed on it and named themselves the Gideons. Why? Because a small group though they were, they could be victorious with God's help.

The group got busy with general evangelical work. In 1908 the idea came: "Aha! We should put a Bible in every hotel room in the United States!"

Two million Bibles later (provided to the hotels by Gideons at no cost), and the Gideons are still (per their website) "telling people about Jesus through associating together for service, sharing personal testimony, and by providing Bibles and New Testaments. While we are often recognized for our work with hotels, we also place and distribute Scriptures in strategic locations so they are available to those who want them, as well as to those who may not know they need them."

This leaves me with two questions:

1. Would Americans go nuts if hotel rooms were stocked with the Qur'an? Answer: Yes, of course.
2. And is it the Gideons' fault that every Little Free Library is infiltrated with religious books? Answer: Them and the Jehovah's Witnesses, I'm guessing.

The Book of Mormon

Marriott hotels have both the Bible and the Book of Mormon in their drawers. *{Not in their pants, in their bedside table drawers. But I like the visual.}*

Marriott's founder, Bill Marriott, was a member of the Church of Latter-day Saints and decided to place the Book of Mormon, alongside the Bible, in all of his hotel rooms.

Marriott hotels are now largely franchised, but the company's franchise agreements include a provision requiring that the Book of Mormon be placed in hotel rooms. The books are paid for by the Marriott Foundation and the Church of the Latter-day Saints.

Marriott locations in some countries, including Vietnam and Indonesia, do not have religious books at all.

Uncrazy Eight

Of the world religions or philosophies I know about, I connect most with Buddhism. Rather than focusing on worshipping one specific God, Buddhists believe in enlightenment (nirvana) through finding inner peace and wisdom. Who doesn't want that?

They believe that suffering is an integral part of life. When we encounter suffering, we can either think and act in a way that creates more suffering or in a way that alleviates the suffering. Our thoughts and actions have consequences, which is the concept of karma. Buddhism is based on four noble truths: suffering, the cause of the suffering, the end of the suffering, and the cause to bring about the end of suffering.

How do you bring about the end of suffering? Through perfecting ethical conduct, ethical discipline, and wisdom.

And how the heck do you do that? By following the Noble Eightfold Path. This path includes the following:

- Right understanding (*Samma ditthi*). Understanding things as they are
- Right thought (*Samma sankappa*). Fostering selfless detachment, love, and nonviolence
- Right speech (*Samma vaca*). Abstaining from lies, divisive speech, abusive speech, and idle chatter
- Right action (*Samma kammanta*). Promoting moral, honorable, and peaceful conduct
- Right livelihood (*Samma ajiva*). Engaging in a profession that is honorable, blameless, and innocent of harm to others
- Right effort (*Samma vayama*). Avoiding the hindrances of sensory desire, ill will, sloth, restlessness, and doubt

- Right mindfulness (*Samma sati*). Engaging in mindful awareness of the body, feelings, the mind, and phenomena
- Right concentration (*Samma samadhi*). Replacing sensations with equanimity and awareness

Through the month, I've gotten a bit of a start on this righting. I've been meditating more and catastrophizing less. I've tried to be more mindful, living in the moment and taking in whatever that moment is bringing. I've intentionally focused on being kind. I've been trying to suppress feelings of anxiousness and replace them with awareness.

I've realized that engaging in curiosities is not a silly indulgence but a critical need. Engaging in the things we long for makes us whole. My curiosity is my soul talking to me, telling me what it needs. I am choosing to nourish it.

And do you know what else? I've been drinking less. Lots less.

But the sloth? Yeah, that needs some work.

!?

All the Words

My days now look quite different from when you and I first met. I'm sleeping well now, usually through the whole night. I'm meditating and journaling regularly. I'm reading and writing daily. I'm exercising . . . oh, shit, I have no adverb to put there because I'm not exercising. Progress, not perfection, folks.

The alcohol is still a work in progress too. I am drinking less often, but I'm still drinking more than I'd like. You know when there are Girl Scout cookies in the pantry and you sit there thinking, "

> Well, maybe I'll just have two more Thin Mints, then save the rest for tomorrow. Actually, three, but that's it. Oh wow, did I just eat the whole sleeve? What does it matter, really, whether I eat the Thin Mints today or tomorrow? Either way the calories are coming in, so fuck it, I'm just going to sit here and eat the whole box.

That's me and wine (also me and Thin Mints).

Rob and I were coordinating calendars yesterday, which involves considering not only our schedules but those of our children, our exes, and our pets. *{I'm not kidding about the pets. Rob has unofficial joint custody of the dogs from his first marriage, so the pups bounce back and forth between houses as if they were offspring.}* All I could think about was wanting wine. Instead I tried to notice my anxiety. *{Hi Pressure-I-Feel-in-My-Chest! I notice you! Welcome.}* I tried to understand the frustration driving it. *{Why do I have to plan around exes and canines? Why can't everything just be about me, me, me, huh?}* And I tried to find a healthier way to manage the feelings. *{Weed, say.}*

So yes, my relationship with alcohol still needs more attention. *{Or perhaps more weed.}*

As I figure out the alcohol thing (or any other thing, for that matter), I'm not going it alone. I've amassed quite a collection of mental health supports—therapist, psychiatrist, primary care physician, husband, family, friends, pizza. And the good thing? They already know what a mess I am, so I don't have to explain. If I were to call a friend and say, "I really think a square of Ghirardelli chocolate, a bottle of Udderly Smooth hand cream, and a flip phone would help me right now," I swear they'd bring me all three. They might wonder, but they'd trust that I had my reasons.

I've thought about my learning focus for this month and have decided to make it "words." Why words? Because they bring me joy. I love thinking about what a word means, where it comes from, and whether it can be preceded by the word "fucking." *{All the best words can. Fucking all the best words can. All the fucking best words can. All the best fucking words can. All the best words fucking can. See?}*

So, let's get to learning. *{And I was kidding about the weed. Mostly.}*

I'm Feeling Perspicacious

I read an article talking about how "truthiness," a word invented by Stephen Colbert, was so perspicacious it was chosen the 2005 word of the year by Merriam-Webster.

I couldn't agree more. It's absolutely perspicacious. In fact, sometimes I feel a little perspicacious myself.

I sound naughty, don't I?

Wait, do I? I have no idea how I sound since I don't know what perspicacious means.

Okay, now I know. I sound "of acute mental vision or discernment." *{That definition is courtesy of Merriam-Webster, my go-to word definition giver throughout this chapter about words (and the whole book, really).}*

You could say I sound shrewd, but that would suggest more "practical, hardheaded cleverness" than perspicacity, which "implies unusual power to see through and comprehend what is puzzling or hidden." Astute is slightly different too, because if you're astute, you're both shrewd and perspicacious, both clever and keen, with a dash of diplomatic.

I think I'm feeling more shrewd than perspicacious, now that I look into it. Clever me.

Fuckity Fuck

I have been doing a lot of writing. *{Including Morning Pages—three pages of handwritten journaling to clear out my mind at the start of the day. I found this recommendation in Julia Cameron's book* It's Never Too Late to Begin Again, *which is full of all sorts of midlife wisdom.}*

I asked Rob to help me cut down a piece—to help me find extra words and slice them out. *{I prefer to use all the words, but some publishers have space constraints, I suppose.}*

Instead, he gave me back a redlined document laden with insightful comments. "Consider the appropriateness of the word 'fuck,'" one comment read.

He explained further when we talked, "You're not Richard Pryor, you know."

Really? I was not aware. "But I do curse rather regularly," I said.

"Yes, but somehow it seems uglier on paper."

Oh, fuck. My writing is full of curse words because I write what I think, and I think in curse words. If I scratch them out, what will I be left with? Pages of prepositions and conjunctions.

I did some checking, to see what other people think. Yup, they agree with Rob. Cursing is more powerful on the page. It's perceived as lazy language, so not appropriate for writing, unless absolutely intentional (for example, in dialogue, if it is language the character would use). Publishers often won't print it. And many readers are simply offended. Generally, cursing in writing is considered gratuitous and bad form.

Fuuuuuuck. Here's the thing. I offend people. I'm not mean or anything (except in my head where, yeah, sometimes I can be a real asshole), but I tend to say inappropriate things at inappropriate times. People who don't like that about me likely won't be reading anything I write. And since you're still reading this many pages in, well, I guess you haven't been too horribly offended or you wouldn't still be here.

There, I considered the appropriateness of the word "fuck," and it's still my favorite.

H-E-Double-Toothpicks

Maybe I could bowdlerize instead of curse—you know, use words like "gosh" and "heck" in the place of the words I really want to use.

Before I can even consider that option, I'd like to know the origin of the word "bowdlerization."

Answer: From Thomas Bowdler, who published a volume of Shakespeare's plays sanitized for those of delicate ear. The internet tells me when you bowdlerize something, you expurgate it by leaving out the vulgar parts.

I hate looking up a definition, only to find that the definition includes another word I don't know so then I have to go look that one up, and then when I look that one up the definition for that one has yet another word I don't understand, and I keep having to look up words until I'm old and tired, not even remembering the original word I wondered about.

Where were we? Bowdlerize means expurgate vulgarity. What's expurgate? To cleanse the bad stuff—like expunge, I suppose.

Fuck it. I'd rather curse.

In Flames

I got a question wrong on a college exam because I didn't understand what the word "infamous" meant. I thought it meant not famous or unknown, but it really means well known for something bad you've done. Why is that?

"Famous" doesn't just mean well known; it also has a positive spin to it—as in, well known for something good you've done. The in- prefix of "infamous" creates the opposite—well known for something bad you've done.

What about the in- prefix of "inflammable"? Why does "inflammable" mean "flammable," when you would think it would mean the opposite—that is, "nonflammable"?

It seems the in- prefix can have several meanings. It can mean "not" (like the word "inactive," meaning "not active") or "toward" or "within" (like the word "inset," meaning "set within").

The word "inflammable" comes from the Latin word *inflammare*—meaning "to inflame." The prefix in the word means "to cause a person or thing to be in or within"—in this case, to cause something to be in flames.

The National Fire Protection Association became concerned that folks would misunderstand the definition of inflammable, such that combustibility warnings would not be understood or heeded. In the early 1920s they encouraged the use of "flammable" instead of "inflammable," to clear up any confusion.

Good thinking.

Clark, Down!

A few days ago my dog jumped up on me as I sat meditating in the living room chair. *{Did you catch that? I'm meditating! Not daily but fairly regularly. Sure, they're only ten-minute meditations, but it's something. So, moderating, journaling, meditating—a self-care trifecta!}*

She's a large dog, so there's simply no room for the two of us. "Clark, down!" I said.

Clark responded from the kitchen, "Really, mom? Now I'm a dog?"

You will recall the dog's name is Miley. Clark is my son.

The kids have been teasing me about this all week. They keep calling me Miley.

I read an article explaining that when you call someone by the wrong name, it suggests you love them. Our brains create a sort of mind map (called a semantic network), grouping related people, places, and things. When you try to remember the name of a loved one, you may retrieve the name of a different loved one whose information is stored nearby in the semantic network. This phenomenon is called misnaming.

Misnaming can occur between pets and children when we see pets as part of the family and thus store information about them along with that of other loved ones.

You see, kids? I'm not a monster.

"I even wrote a piece about how much I love Miley," I said to Clark.

"Did you write a piece about how much you love me?" he asked.

"Ummmm."

Well, now I know what my next piece will be about!

The Sarcasm Font

I saw a post complaining that the world needs a sarcasm font. "It could replace Comic Sans!" I replied sarcastically, but since I didn't have a sarcasm font, perhaps confusingly.

Comic Sans is a notoriously hated font. It was designed in 1994 by typographer Vincent Connare, who intended the font to be used in thought bubbles or children's materials. When it is used in official documents, it seems silly. Here, I'll show you:

> The unanimous Declaration of the thirteen united States of America, When in the Course of human events, it becomes necessary for one people to dissolve the political bands which have connected them with another, and to assume among the powers of the earth, the separate and equal station to which the Laws of Nature and of Nature's God entitle them, a decent respect to the opinions of mankind requires that they should declare the causes which impel them to the separation.

It's hard to take even the Declaration of Independence seriously in Comic Sans. But yes, I agree, there should be a sarcasm font.

On the internet, some folks mark sarcasm with the tilde. I've never done that, because ~ I'm so hip ~ (with tildes, because I'm so not). Lowercase letters can also be used to show snark, for example, "lucie is so hip." Adding a period can show attitude—"OK. Fine." is feistier than "Okay, fine." Some people type /s at the end of a sentence to indicate sarcasm, but that seems like a joke killer.

There have been efforts to develop a sarcasm font. Sartalics is an italics font but with the italics leaning left instead of right. It's not a Unicode font though (so not readily available on your operating system), so it didn't catch on.

Well, until they figure it out, I guess we have regular old italics, which are ~ so useful. ~ /s.

I Forgot Perscipacious Again

I forgot what the word "perscipacious" means again. I wrote about it before, but now I've forgotten, so I am going to have to look it up again. Probably thirty more times before I remember it.

Whoops. Let's start with this: the word is not "per*scipa*cious." It's "per*spic*acious." I had best not try to use it publicly until I get that down. Of course, knowing what it means would help too.

Here's the refresher. "Of acute mental vision or discernment. Keen." Oh, yeah, not feeling too keen for not remembering that word.

The Worst Kind of Dictionary

Now that I'm paying particular mind to all of the words I don't know, I realize that my vocabulary is lacking. If I have a different entry for every word I don't know, this will become a dictionary and not even an alphabetized one, which seems like the least useful kind of dictionary.

I'm going to consolidate some of the words here, giving you a taster instead of a full unalphabetized dictionary—like an amuse-bouche of vocabulary, except not tasty.

Liminal: barely perceptible; or in between/ transitional. I thought that word meant "spiritual," but it turns out I was thinking of numinous.

Abstemious: using restraint in eating or drinking. How is that different from abstinent? Abstemious means you are moderate in food and drink, while abstinent means you abstain altogether.

Didactic: intended to teach, especially moralistically. I knew the word "didactic" meant teachy, but I didn't quite know the word meant preachy. Good to know it has an angle.

Solipsistic: egocentric. You know those words you look up and when you do, you're like, "Oh yeeeeeeeeah. I knew that." Solipsistic is one of those I-have-to-look-it-up-every-single-fucking-time words. I'm going to try to remember it like this. "Sol" means alone or self, so you're self-sistic, which sounds an awful lot like self-centric. Quiz me on this one when you see me next.

Discomfit: I think it means to make someone uncomfortable, as in discomfort, but if it did, why wouldn't they just say "discomfort"? It must mean something else. Actually, in today's usage, discomfit and discomfort mean the same thing—to cause uncomfortableness—though discomfit is usually used as a verb and discomfort as a noun.

Sartorial: My wild guess is this word comes from Sartre, the French philosopher, so it means "thinky"—because that's a word (except it's not). Absolutely wrong. It means related to a tailor or tailored clothes and comes from *sartor*, which is tailor in Latin.

Perfidious: disloyal, traitorous, liary-liary-pants-on-firery. Use it in a sentence, you say? The "friend" who told me bangs would look good on me was perfidious.

Exegesis: Exposition, critical interpretation. Something we all want to avoid. If you see the word "exegesis," run. It's gonna be boring.

Sardonic: Biting, snarky. Well, that's a word you'd think I'd know. /s

Internecine: Seems like "necine" should mean something about being born, so I'm guessing internecine means "born between" or "born within"? Nope. It means mutually destructive.

Solecism: A verbal stumble or a breach of etiquette. If you're wondering, solecism is not the same word as solipsism, which you may recall means either extreme egotism or "a theory holding that the self can know nothing but its own modifications and that the self is the only existent thing" (whatever the heck that means).

Sanguine: I always feel like this should mean "bloody" (because *sangre* in Spanish is blood), but I think it may mean contemplative. Fuck. Wrong again. It can mean "of or related to blood," but the primary definition is "confidently optimistic."

Exegesis: I don't know where I heard it, but the word is written in my notepad with a question mark next to it. Oh, shit, I just realized I looked this up and wrote about it a few lines up. Here we go again, for my sieve of a brain: "exegesis"

is a long-winded explanation. My brain protected me from the boredom of an exegesis by
allowing me to forget that word. Thank you,
brain. You were right on this one.

It's Thor's Day

I'm having such fun focusing on words this month. Too
much fun maybe, because I've holed myself in the house
reading and writing. But you know what's different about
me now? I recognize when I'm isolating and know it's time
to connect.

I called Mama to schedule lunch. She suggested we get
together on Thursdee.

"How about todee instead?" I asked.

"What?"

"Instead of lunch Thursdee, let's just go todee."

"Very funny, Lucie."

I like to tease her about her days of the week, which she
calls: Mondee, Tuesdee, Wednesday, Thursdee, Friday, Saturday, Sundee. I understand the twang, but I'll never understand the inconsistency.

I'll also never understand why she makes two-syllable
words out of one-syllable words (yay-yus instead of yes) but
one-syllable words out of two-syllable words (mare instead
of mirror). I speak Texan, but she speaks Tay-yuk-sun.

The conversation made me curious. Why is Thursday
called Thursday? Because it was named after Thor, the Norse
god of thunder—so it's Thor's Day. In Romance languages
that day of the week is named after Jupiter, the Roman god
of sky and thunder, and thus the *j* starts the words: *jueves*
(Spanish), *jeudi* (French), *dies Jovis* (Latin).

The other days of the week?

Monday. Named after the moon (the moon's day)
Tuesday. Named for the Nordic god of war, Tiu or Tyr
Wednesday. Named after Woden, the Nordic god of the wild hunt
Friday. Named for Freya, the goddess of love
Saturday. Named after Saturn
Sunday. Named after the sun

But understanding Mama? That's for another dee.

Also, I Can't Spell

In addition to not knowing what words mean, it seems I also don't know how many of them are spelled. Here are some entries designed to save you spelling embarrassment.

Guttural: I was sure the word for a growly sound was "gutteral"—like from the gutter, I suppose. It's "guttural"—like from the throat (*guttur* in Latin).

Intelligentsia: It's not "intelligensia" but "intelligentsia." It has a *t* in it. Who knew? Probably the members of it. And just in case you need a refresher, "intelligentsia" means a group of intelligent and well-educated people who guide the political, artistic, or social development of their society.

Lambaste: I just realized the word (to verbally attack) has an *e* on the end—which looks right when spelled, but I suspect if I were in the spelling bee I'd lose on that one.

Genealogy: I always thought it was "gene-ology." I just found out I was misspelling it, because *no one bothered to tell me* over the past five decades.

Duplication Duplication

Do you see what I did right there with this entry title? I duplicated. Twice. So I reduplicated.

Regular old reduplication is a repeated word or word part—knock-knock and bye-bye, for example.

Ablaut reduplication is a similar concept, but the second word or word part is repeated with a changed vowel—singsong, for example. What's interesting is that the first of these always has the letter *i* as its vowel and the second has either an *a* or an *o* as its vowel. Did that just happen by magic, or did the word elves do it for us?

chitchat	jibber jabber	riffraff
crisscross	jinglejangle	singsong
dillydally	King Kong	splish-splash
ding-dong	knickknack	ticktack
flimflam	mishmash	ticktock
flip-flop	ping-pong	tip-top
hip-hop	pitter-patter	zigzag

Cum To

Whenever I see the word "cum" outside of the phrase "cum laude," I cringe. For some reason if "cum" is followed by another Latin word, I read it as "coom" and thus do not cringe. But follow an English word with the word "cum," and I'm uncomfortable.

When we are using the word "cum" in the non-semen sense, why is it spelled that way? Couldn't they cum up with another spelling?

The answer, of course, is the word is Latin for "with" and means "along with being." *{And the Latin word, you may guess, predates its ejaculatory homonym.}*

So a shop-cum-workshop is both a shop and a workshop.

This exposes another thing I did not know. I always thought the hyphenated "cum" meant "become." In the example above, it would be a shop that had evolved into a workshop.

It appears I don't know shit about cum.

Ooday Ouyay Eakspay Igpay Atinlay

Did you know you can hire someone to invent a language for you? The Language Creation Society—whose cofounder David Peterson created the Dothraki language for *Game of Thrones*—has a job board where you can post your need. The society even suggests payment amounts ranging from $100 (inventing the sound of the language and two dozen names in the language) to $800 (inventing the sound of the language, grammar, five hundred words, and twenty sample sentences).

An invented language is called a "constructed language" or "conlang." When the constructed language is invented for artistic purposes, such as Dothraki, Klingon (used in *Star Trek*), or Elvish (used in J. R. R. Tolkien's Middle-earth), it is called an "artistic language" or "artlang." Conlangs designed for international communication, such as Esperanto, are called "auxiliary languages" or "auxlangs."

Interestingly, sign language is not considered a conlang. Because it evolved over time, without conscious planning, it is considered a natural language.

And pig latin? It's not considered a conlang either, because it's not a complete invented language but a transformation of the English language. It is considered a language game—where language is altered playfully using some defined rule.

In Spanish such language games are called *jerigonzas*. When I was a kid in Mexico, we played one where we repeated the vowel sound of each syllable, adding an *f*. So *hola* became "hofolafa." My sister and I used the same methodology on English words, turning "hello" to "hefelofo." And if we were feeling particularly playful, we'd pair the *f* game and pig latin, so "bullshit" would become "ullfullshitfitbayfay." Oh, the lengths to which children will go to curse.

Beware the Thespians

When I was reading about conlangs, I learned about Silbo Gomero, the language used on the island of La Gomera, one of the Spanish Canary Islands. Silbo Gomero is a whistled language that transposes whistle tones for the spoken sounds of the Spanish language. The whistles carry better across the island's ravines and valleys, allowing for effective communication where there is no cell phone coverage.

Did you know in some countries, including Turkey, whistling at night is thought to summon the devil? And in some places, including Russia, whistling indoors is thought to bring poverty. Of course, if you whistle in a theater you're just begging for bad luck, and a horde of thespians will probably pounce.

Curious what other things are bad luck to say or do in the theater? So was I.

- Mentioning *Macbeth*
- Saying "Good luck"
- Leaving shoes on a table
- Bringing a pet, a peacock feather, or a mirror on stage
- Lighting a trio of candles
- Turning off the ghost light (the single light always left burning)
- Giving a performer flowers before the show

Good grief, thespians are a superstitious bunch. What do they really have to worry about? It's not like these are dangerous things, like stepping on cracks, opening umbrellas indoors, or having sex before marriage.

Perscipascious? Prescipacious?

Dead serious, I've forgotten this word again. Why the hell can I not remember how to spell or pronounce this word, and what it means? It's like I have a chastity belt on my brain keeping this word out.

Okay, here I go, looking it up again, while you sit there giggling. Perspicacious: of acute mental vision or discernment: keen

I'm going to remember it this way. It's like perspire. Perspi. And sweating gives you a keen smell. I'll get back to you the next time I come across the word to see how the sweating thing worked for me. By the way, what I just did there is a connection mnemonic (memory aid). There are also other types of mnemonics.

- Image mnemonics (visual aids)
- Music mnemonics (for example, the ABC song). *{Did you hear they changed the tune a bit at the lmnop part? Google it. It's completely disturbing.}*
- Name mnemonics (taking the first letter of each word and making something memorable of it—like "Every Good Boy Does Fine" and "All Cows Eat Grass" to remember the notes on the music staves. *{And how the hell did I just now learn that the plural of staff in the musical context is "staves" not "staffs"?}*
- Name of expression mnemonics (you use the first letter of each thing you want to remember and make another word of it)

- Organization or outline mnemonics (you organize or outline a topic helping you remember)

You might think my bad memory is wine related, but it's not. I'm doing a great job managing alcohol consumption, and by that, I mean I'm not drinking! For right now. I'm not saying I'll never drink again, but I figured it was time for a break.

That's the good news. The bad news? I've been going to sleep when I get stressed. It seems that I have two ways of coping with stress—impairment and sleep. Just those two. Rob is hoping I'll add sex as a third way, but I think meditation is probably safer. Sure, the sex would be great in the short term, but if Rob is ever out of town, am I going to run out and sleep with the whole metroplex?

Though I joke, I am concerned. I've mentioned that over the years, I've coped with anxiety in the following ways: overworking, oversleeping, overdrinking, overshopping, overeating, overexercising, and most recently, over–*90 Day Fiancé*-ing. I've just been too busy to notice the overages. Now that my life is less frenetic I have the time, the insight, and the energy to develop healthier skills. So yes, I'm focusing on words this month, but I'm also focusing on me.

Sherpa, Sherpa

Last night I babysat my nephew James. He's just over a year old. If he were my baby, I would be able to tell you exactly how many months and weeks. But he's my nephew, so for now it's just good I remember his name.

Being as young as he is, James goes to bed early, which left lots of TV time. Among other things, I watched John Oliver's show. I forgot how funny and learny-interesting that show is.

Oliver did a piece about sherpas. He went through the moral concern about wealthy, inexperienced climbers hiring sherpas to do the extremely dangerous job of getting them to the top of Mount Everest and paying the sherpas sums that sherpas couldn't earn in any other position—that is, giving them offers of dangerous employment that they just can't refuse. *{The average cost of a Mount Everest climb is $45,000, of which $5,000 is paid to the sherpa.}*

Having never thought about climbing such a mountain, I had not thought about the associated moral issues.

Oliver also noted that "sherpa" is a capitonym, a word that changes its meaning when capitalized. Capital Sherpa is an ethnic group living in Nepal. Lowercase sherpa is a worker who helps haul rich white men up the mountain.

Other capitonyms include these:

- August (the month) vs. august (majestic)
- Cancer (the constellation) vs. cancer (the disease)
- Catholic (the religion) vs. catholic (universal)
- Lent (when you give up chocolate, cursing, or God forbid both) vs. lent (past tense of lend)
- March (the month) vs. march (walk)
- May (the month) vs. may (might)
- Polish (from Poland) vs. polish (shine up)

Polish and polish, you will note, are spelled the same but pronounced differently. Those are called heteronyms. So Polish/polish is both a capitonym and a heteronym.

Wait, so what are homographs and homophones and homonyms? I have these all mixed up.

Homonyms and homophones are two words that sound the same but have different meanings.

- Homonyms: Umbrella term. Words with the same sound but different meanings, whether they are spelled the same or differently. Examples: fair (county) and fair (reasonable); pair (couple) and pear (fruit)
- Homophones: A subset of homonyms. Words with the same sound, but different meanings and different spellings: Example: pair and pear.

Homographs and heteronyms are words with the same spelling, but with different meanings.

- Homographs: Umbrella term. Words with the same spelling but with different meanings, whether they are pronounced the same or differently. Examples: lie (untruth) and lie (recline); tear (rip) and tear (eye juice)
- Heteronyms: A subset of homographs. Words with the same spelling but with different meanings and different pronunciations. Example: tear (rip) and tear (eye juice)

Dear God, I hope I don't ever get quizzed on this. There's no way this learning is going to stick.

Period Space Space
I know the youngsters find it annoying when the oldsters use two spaces after a period. I know we don't need two spaces anymore, but why exactly? I think it has something to do with the fact that we don't use typewriters anymore, but why did we need two spaces on typewriters and only one on computers?

Apparently typewriters used monospaced fonts, which gave the same amount of space to each letter—whether it was the skinny *i* or the wide *w*. That left a lot of blank space in the sentence. In order to make it clear that a full stop was needed, people used two spaces after a period.

Computers use proportional spacing, giving more space to the *w* than to the *i*. Because of this, there is not extra space after the skinny letters. A single space after a period is sufficient visual notice of the full stop.

Well, shoot. Now I'm going to have to replace all of my double spaces with single. And I don't know if it's a habit I can break. Sorry, editors!

What the Graf?

I learned that in the editorial world, the word "graf" means paragraph, which of course it does. In looking that up, I found a few other editorial terms I didn't know. *{Yes, it's embarrassing that I had to look that up, but I wanted to be sure it wasn't something trickier than a mere paragraph, which it wasn't. And I saved you the embarrassment of feeling foolish, in case you were thinking it might be something trickier than a mere paragraph, which it isn't.}*

- 30. A number indicating the end of the story (likely coming from Western Union's telegraph code, where the 30 meant end).
- Bastard title. The first page of the book, which includes the title but no subtitle, author's name, etc. *{And here I thought a bastard title was "Senator from the Great State of Texas."}*
- Corrigendum. An error discovered after a book has been printed and corrected by addendum.
- Folio. Page number (and drop folios are page numbers at the bottom of the page). *{So, if you remove the page numbers, do you exfoliate them?}*

- Kern. To adjust the space between letters.
- Rule. A line across the page (vertical or horizontal).
- Signpost. A cross reference to something referred to in another part of the text.
- TK. Abbreviation for material "to come."

Glad I know this stuff now, or I'd be screwed when I try to get this published so you can read it. They'd put "30" at the end of the book, and I'd be like "There's a mistake!" and I'd cross it out, and then they'd add it in, and I'd cross it out. It would be never-fucking-ending.

Getting Some Zzzzs

I ran across two Z words I didn't know. How often does a Z word come up at all—and then one you don't know? I mean, there's "zoo" and "zebra," and that's about it, right?

Wrong. There's "zarzuela."

It came up like this. Mackenzie texted from Spain asking if I'd be willing to buy her a ticket to the opera. Normally a kid would ask for a sweatshirt, but okay. She decided she'd like to go to *Doña Franciquista*, which is a Spanish zarzuela. Mackenzie described it like this: "It's an early twentieth-century style of opera incorporating some spoken scene and dance with operatic singing." Yeah, she's a weird kid. That's why I love her.

Then there's "zarf."

I'm reading A. J. Jacobs's book *Thanks a Thousand: A Gratitude Journey*, in which he tracks down and thanks the many people involved in making his morning cup of coffee. One of the things he is thankful for is the zarf. That's the technical term for the coffee sleeve. The word comes from the Arabic word *zarf*, which means container or envelope. Zarves were the ornamental metal (or wood or whatever) protectors they slipped cups in, since cups didn't have handles and would otherwise scald you.

In the early 1990s attorney Jay Sorenson invented the cardboard ones, calling them Java Jackets. He sold them at coffee conventions, and now, they're everywhere.

Thank you, Jay Sorenson. I too am grateful.

Be on the lookout for the Z words, folks. They're handy to have in a game of Scrabble.

I suppose the Zs are a good place to end this month of words. What a good month it has been! Perfect? No. But dang, it's been fun. Reading, writing, connecting, meditating, moderating, cursing. You know how I feel? Perspicacious. Perfectly perspicacious.

All the Other Things

It's the twelfth month after retirement, and I couldn't be more at peace with my life. Remember when all I did was watch reality television? When all I wanted for my life was wine? When I didn't know the word "perspicacious"? I've got that shit nailed now.

Throughout the year I've wondered about things that didn't fall into my monthly focus. Did I look into them? Of course. I'm not a Central Park horse. I don't have blinders. But I must confess I often looked into them with a side thought—"Is there some way this could fit into my focus for the month?" This month I'm letting my curiosity run free, just any little thing I'm curious about.

For example, yesterday as Rob and I were in the car, I said, "Why do they call it a glove box?"

"Because it's for gloves?" Rob said.

"Yeah, but is there anything else to it?"

"Is that a rhetorical question? Are you just musing again, or do you really expect me to answer?"

"Oh, I expect you to answer. I demand it, in fact."

Rob ignored me, like he's gotten so good at doing.

When we got home I looked it up, then proudly announced my findings. "There's more to it. In the olden days, when lots of cars were convertibles, drivers had gloves to keep their hands from going numb in the cold."

"Right, so the glove box is for gloves," Rob said.

"Yes, but they're *super important* gloves."

Rob shook his head.

But that little bit of learning was fun for me. It was a small curiosity that taught me something. A world-changing something? No, but it added a bit of color to my understanding. It made me happy, and that's enough.

When you pay attention—really, really pay attention— you can't go five minutes without coming across something you don't know and can annoy your mate by asking. Well, maybe you can go five minutes, but I can't. Maybe you're smarter. Or maybe you don't have to let every passing thought escape through your mouth. Or maybe you don't even have a mate to annoy.

I guess I thought I would know most everything by the time I hit my fifties. Or that I wouldn't know nearly enough but would no longer be capable of learning because my mind had been made mush by kids and work. But now that I have more free time and energy, I have space to notice all the things I do not know. I can have a passing wonder about glove boxes and spend my whole day learning about them, if I'm so inclined (I'm not).

Anyway, this chapter is a hodgepodge of my curiosities.

Oh, and one final thing. Did you know that in British English, the word is "hotchpotch" instead of "hodgepodge"? It's like they're from another country or something.

Hand Cuffing

It's January, and I've come across my first curiosity of the new year: I read that the first Sunday in January is the biggest day for online dating signups—even bigger than cuffing season. Makes sense, with it being "new year, new you" time, but what the heck is cuffing season?

It's the time of the year starting in the fall when the weather gets blustery and gals and guys (or gals and gals, or guys and guys, or nonbinary and—let's just say people)—when *people* want to snuggle up. Maybe they want someone to take home for the holidays. Maybe they'd like someone to kiss at the stroke of the new year or to take out on Valentine's Day. Maybe they're just itching for a fight. Whatever the maybe, it's a popular time of year to pair up. *{Cuffing season is not a term of BDSM origin, if you're wondering. Rather it seems to be a phrase born on Twitter, as so many clever phrases were.}*

Makes sense to me. I've heard that August is typically the biggest month for baby births. That would put it at a November conception for a full-term baby. So it seems to be a popular time for coupling all around.

The VP's House

"I have a really stupid question," I said to Rob.

"Go ahead."

"Where does the vice president live? And how do I not know that?"

"Is it Blair House?" he said.

"I don't know. Shouldn't we know this?"

"Yes, yes, we absolutely should."

The vice president lives at Number One Observatory Circle, on the grounds of the US Naval Observatory.

In 1966, after President Kennedy's assassination, Congress passed a law designating this property for use as the vice president's residence, and a new house was to be built. Pending construction, Vice Presidents Humphrey, Agnew, and Ford lived in their private homes (as did the prior vice presidents), with security upgrades made by the Secret Service.

In 1974 the house still hadn't been built, and Congress passed a law making the Admiral's House on the property the temporary residence of the vice president. Vice President Rockefeller was given access to this house, though he used it primarily for entertainment purposes, preferring to live in his private residence. *{I guess if you're Rockefeller, your thirty-room mansion on twenty-five acres in prime DC beats the digs the American populace can afford to provide for you.}*

In 1977 Vice President Walter Mondale moved into the home. Every vice president since has lived in this residence.

In 1991 the Navy concluded that Congress would never have the new house built, and it moved forward with extensive renovations to the Admiral's House. The residence is located 2.3 miles from the US Capitol and 2.8 miles from the White House.

What is Blair House, if not the VP's residence? Blair House, along with Lee House, Peter Parker House (no relation), and 704 Jackson Place, is the president's guest house, primarily used by visiting dignitaries and guests of the president. Blair House is located on Pennsylvania Avenue, across the street from the White House.

That's all good information, but none of it answers my fundamental question: How the hell did I not know that?

Them's Bad Odds

Did you know that almost 20 percent of US presidents have died in office? If I were offered a position with good benefits but a one-in-five chance of croaking on the job, I'd decline the offer.

Of the eight who died, four were assassinated while in office—Abraham Lincoln (1865), James Garfield (1881), William McKinley (1901), and John F. Kennedy (1963).

William Harrison was the first president to die in office, in 1841, only thirty-two days into his presidency, from a cold that turned into pneumonia.

Zachary Taylor died in 1850, sixteen months into his presidency, of some sort of gastrointestinal ailment. In 1991 his body was exhumed so testing could be done to determine if he had actually died of arsenic poisoning. He hadn't, so they popped him right back in his box.

William Harding died in 1923, twenty-nine months into his presidency. He was visiting San Francisco when he had a fatal heart attack in his room at the Palace Hotel.

Franklin Roosevelt was the last president to die of natural causes in office. He died in 1945, not even three months into his fourth term, of a cerebral hemorrhage.

Wait! How the hell did I not know that Franklin Roosevelt was in office for that long?! He was president from March 1933 to April 1945.

In March 1947 Congress approved the Twenty-Second Amendment, and in 1951 it was finally ratified by the states. The Twenty-Second Amendment provides that a president cannot be elected for more than two terms of office. And if a person becomes president without being elected and has served in the position for more than two years, that person can only be elected for one more term.

My knowledge gaps are getting truly embarrassing. Oh, and to make me feel even worse about myself, I just had to look up how to spell "embarrassing," because I thought it should have one *r* in it like "harassing."

Keys to the Kingdom

A friend heard an interview (on NPR, I'm guessing, because that's where all of my friends hang out) about a guy who broke into apartment buildings using universal elevator keys. I didn't realize there was such a thing.

The Safety Code for Elevators and Escalators requires that elevators have a common key for fire safety purposes.

For newer elevators this key is the FEO-K1 key. Older elevators may have different keys, which must be kept on site in a lockbox accessible to firefighters. Some states have different key requirements, but a clever criminal could identify the particular key required for your state and keep that one on his key ring. *{Of course, elevator access would only get the bad guy to your floor. He'd have to use a whole 'nother trick to get into your actual apartment. My guess is he goes with pizza delivery.}*

Is purchase of the FEO-K1 key restricted to fire service or elevator personnel? Yes, were it not for the internet, where anyone can buy Christmas sweaters, tooth whitener, or universal elevator keys. So I guess buildings shouldn't consider elevators as much of a help with security.

This reminds me of the CAT key, a universal key for Caterpillar heavy equipment. Other heavy equipment brands like Case and John Deere have universal keys of their own. The thinking is that operators on construction sites should be able to operate all the equipment without having to keep up with individual keys.

That makes sense, but doesn't the risk of theft outweigh that convenience? Some lenders and insurance companies think so and require that after-market antitheft devices be installed. And many manufacturers install GPS tracking on the equipment so it can be hunted down if stolen. Newer models often have access by keypad or thumbprint, and insurance companies will give you a reduction on your rates if you have an access device like that. But there are also old-fashioned ways to protect the equipment, such as lining it up head-to-tail overnight, making it harder to steal equipment in the middle of the line.

Want to know something else interesting? Equipment dealers often have parts drop boxes throughout their territory. Dealers deliver orders to these drop boxes on regular

All the Other Things

225

runs, keeping customers from having to drive all the way to the dealer to pick up their parts. How do customers access these boxes? With their universal keys. Couldn't one customer steal another's order? Sure, but since most folks in this world are honorable, it seldom happens.

Keep all of this to yourself, would you? I just compromised all sorts of safety.

With the Force of Gale

Today's curiosity: What are gale force winds? I know they're strong winds, but how strong exactly? Can any strong wind be called gale force, or is it some particular wind speed?

It's specific. In 1805 Sir Francis Beaufort of the Royal Navy made a scale to measure wind speeds.

Gale force winds: Sustained winds of 34–40 knots.

Strong gale force wi—

Sorry, quick interruption so I can remind myself what a knot is.

Answer: It's the speed of one nautical mile per hour.

But ummm, sorry, another quick question. What's a nautical mile?

Answer: It's a distance equal to one minute of latitude.

Okay, got it. But wait. What's a minute of latitude?

Answer: A degree of latitude is divided into sixty minutes of latitude. So it's one-sixtieth of a degree of latitude.

Are you starting to see why it takes me forever to learn anything?

Answer: I started to see that a long, long time ago.

May I ask one more question?

Answer: Fine.

How many degrees of latitude are there?

Answer: 180. Latitudes are the imaginary lines running east/west across the globe. The equator is at 0 degrees latitude. There are 90 degrees of latitude between the equator and each pole. And to save you from having to ask (because I know you will), the distance between the North and South Pole is 12,436 miles, so each degree of latitude is 12,436 miles / 180 degrees = 69 miles from the next.

Got it.

Answer: I'm not done. Remember when I said a minute of latitude is one-sixtieth of a degree of latitude? That means each minute of latitude is one-sixtieth of 69 miles or 1.15 miles. A nautical mile is equal to that distance: 1.15 miles.

Okay.

Answer: Still not done. A knot, then, is a speed of 1.15 mph. So when we say gale force winds have sustained winds of 34–40 knots, that equates to 39–46 mph.

I'm with you.

Answer: Good. You may continue on with the Beaufort scale of wind speeds then.

Okay, so in 1805, Sir Francis Beaufort of the Royal Navy made a scale to measure wind speeds.

- Gale force winds: Sustained winds of 34–40 knots (39–46 mph). The effect of these winds on water is described as "moderately high (18–25 feet) waves of greater length, edges of crests begin to break into spin-drift, foam blown in streaks." On land, "twigs breaking off trees, generally impedes progress."
- Strong gale force winds: Sustained winds of 41–47 knots (47–54 mph). At this speed, you can expect on water "high waves (23–32 feet), sea begins to roll, dense streaks of foam, spray may reduce visibility." On land, "slight structural damage occurs, slate blows off roofs."
- Storm: Sustained winds of 48–55 knots (55–63 mph): On water, you can expect "very high waves (29–41

feet) with overhanging crests, sea white with densely blown foam, heaving rolling, lowered visibility." On land, trees will be uprooted and there will be significant structural damage.

- Violent storm: Sustained winds of 56–63 knots (64–72 mph). On water, there will be "exceptionally high waves (37–52 feet), foam patches cover sea, visibility more reduced." On land, there will be "widespread damage."
- Hurricane: Sustained winds of 64+ knots (73+ mph). On water, "air filled with foam, waves over 45 feet, sea completely white with driving spray, visibility greatly reduced."

Since I mentioned hurricanes, I'm curious about something: Do they give both traditionally male and traditionally female names to hurricanes these days?

Since 1979, yes, they do.

In the early 1950s, the National Hurricane Center revisited its naming protocol. At the time, hurricanes were named in the order of the Combined Communications Board spelling alphabet, with the first hurricane of the season named Able, the second Baker, the third Charlie, etc. The names were repeated each year, which the National Hurricane Center decided was confusing.

In 1953 the National Hurricane Center revised the system so that names would not repeat. They decided all hurricanes would be named with female names, following the naval practice of referring to storms in the feminine.

In 1979 the system was again revised, giving tropical storms and hurricanes both traditionally male and traditionally female names. The names are now preassigned, with the list repeating every six years. Names can be removed from the list for cultural or historical reasons (e.g., Katrina, removed in 2005).

Wouldn't it be grand if we got to the point that names weren't considered male or female? That we all just got names instead of gendered names? I should have led the charge on this, but I wasn't much of a feminist in my childbearing years. Come to think of it, I wasn't much of anything in my childbearing years—except tired. Very, very tired.

Who Invented ChapStick?

I'm hooked on ChapStick. I bet I'm dehydrated.

Who invented ChapStick, anyway? A physician named Charles Brown Fleet in the 1880s.

And now, a rabbit hole. ChapStick is becoming a genericized brand—that is, a brand so popular its name is now known as the generic, risking its trademark protection.

Brand names that have lost trademark protection for being genericized include Aspirin, Cellophane, Dry Ice, Escalator, Flip Phone, Heroin, Kerosene, Lanolin, Laundromat, Linoleum, Teleprompter, Thermos, Trampoline, and Videotape. *{Who was marketing Heroin? Bayer, as a cough suppressant and morphine substitute.}*

What can a brand do to keep people from using the brand name to describe the whole category of product? Band-Aid fights it by adding the word "brand" in its ads ("I am stuck on Band-Aid brand"), as has Jell-o ("Jell-o brand gelatin"). Xerox fights it by using its product category after its name ("Use a Xerox copier" instead of "xerox this"). Lego has also used the product category approach ("Lego Bricks" vs. "Legos"). Velcro made a music video asking people to call its product hook-and-loop. It's a fun video, titled "Don't Say Velcro," if you want to YouTube it.

See how I did that? Used YouTube as a verb? YouTube doesn't like that, just like Google doesn't. Brand names should never be used as a verb or noun, to protect the brand.

Having various products in your line-up helps protect the brand too. Band-Aid, for example, makes a host of wound-care products.

It must be hard to get too big for your britches.

Speaking of feeling too big for your britches, I fear I have done that. I was feeling so confident in the new, postretirement, intellectually engaged, moderately drinking, meditating, writerly me that I've had a setback.

I submitted a piece for publication and just got a rejection. I've grown accustomed to rejection (as all writers must), but I was so sure the piece was both fabulous and a great fit for the publication that this one stings.

I'm spinning in self-doubt now. The editor probably hates my writing. He wishes I would quit submitting to him because everything I send is terrible. Maybe he doesn't even read it, since there's no use bothering. Worse yet, he probably does read it because he's kind, but then he feels sorry for me. He thinks I'm a bit pathetic. He's hoping a friend will tell me to quit writing, because I'm really no good at it. He'd like to tell me himself, but he can't bear to crush my soul.

Gosh, this busy editor sure is spending a lot of time thinking about me, a person he's never even met, don't you think? I don't know whether to be flattered or scared. *{This is one of those times when a sarcasm font would come in handy.}*

The Color of Weird

I'm reading Michelle Obama's memoir, *Becoming*. In it, she mentions the weird names crayons had when she was a child. Now I'm curious. What were those weird names? I feel like I remember ecru, but what else? Let's say in 1972, at the height of my crayon use, what colors would the sixty-four-crayon box have included?

Ready? Because she's right. There were some weird-ass colors. Oh, and ecru wasn't one of them.

Apricot	Green-Yellow	Raw Umber
Aquamarine	Indian Red	Red
Bittersweet	Lavender	Red-Orange
Black	Lemon Yellow	Red-Violet
Blue	Magenta	Salmon
Blue-Gray	Mahogany	Sea Green
Blue-Green	Maize	Sepia
Blue-Violet	Maroon	Silver
Brick Red	Melon	Sky Blue
Brown	Midnight Blue	Spring
Burnt Orange	Mulberry	Tan
Burnt Sienna	Navy Blue	Thistle
Cadet Blue	Olive Green	Turquoise Blue
Carnation Pink	Orange	Violet
Copper	Orange-Red	Violet-Blue
Cornflower	Orange-Yellow	Violet-Red
Forest Green	Orchid	White
Gold	Peach	Yellow
Goldenrod	Periwinkle	Yellow-Green
Gray	Pine Green	Yellow-Orange
Green	Plum	
Green-Blue	Raw Sienna	

And since we're on the subject of weirdness, let's talk about me a bit, shall we?

My freak-out about the rejection was overdone. Obviously the editor isn't spending a single minute of his time thinking about me. There are so many reasons my piece could have been rejected. It might not have had the right voice for the publication. The editor might not have had room to publish it. It might have been too similar to something he's run before. It might not have tickled his fancy. He might automatically reject every third piece he receives on the second Thursday of the month. There are a zillion reasons the essay could have been rejected, and about zero of those are personal.

So how did I get to that peace? Well, first, I wanted to drink a beer, and I didn't. Yay, me! I decided to notice my discomfort and sit with it. It's okay for me to feel uncomfortable. I don't have to kill that feeling with booze or sleep every time it comes.

Then I meditated. I was still anxious, so I journaled. I still felt anxious. And I decided it was fine. A bit of anxiety wouldn't kill me.

And then I started reading and got curious about crayon colors. And now the anxiety is gone. Poof! And I'm fine. Just fine.

This curiosity project is really something.

Who Is Occam?

Who is Occam? And what's with his razor?

Answer: If there are two plausible explanations for something, the one that is simplest or that requires the least number of assumptions is probably the correct one. The theory is named after William of Ockham, a friar who posited that "more things should not be used than necessary."

Here's where I can put this in practice. Yesterday Clark texted asking if he could leave school early. I said no. Then, feeling suspicious he might have already left school or would soon be leaving despite what I had said, I looked up his phone on Find My Phone (which had been activated after a recent not-where-he-was-supposed-to-be infraction). His phone wasn't listed. Options:

1. He made his phone go dark with teen magic, so I wouldn't know he had left school.
2. I was looking at the wrong tab on the Find My iPhone app.

Ding ding! You win. The easiest answer is that Mom doesn't know how to work a damn phone and falsely accused son of wrongdoing. Whoops. Sorry, son.

She's Home!

Mackenzie came home for a visit. We weren't even off airport property when she told me stuff I didn't know.

First, she said that overinflating your tires will make your car 5 to 10 percent more fuel efficient. The thinking is that if an underinflated tire makes the car hard to propel, then an overinflated one must make it easier, requiring less fuel to move the vehicle.

As it happens though, it's mostly untrue, despite the authority with which Mackenzie declared it. You can't overinflate the tire enough to make a real difference. Besides, overinflation affects tire wear and safety, so it's a bad idea. That said, making sure your tires aren't underinflated is helpful.

Second, Mackenzie said overinflating your tires slows down your odometer. The reasoning: larger tires require fewer rotations to go the same distance.

Apparently that's somewhat true, though most reports say you can't make the tires big enough to make any meaningful difference.

So two minutes of contact with Mackenzie, and two factoids debunked.

I'm so glad she's home. *{No sarcasm font needed. I'm really, really glad.}*

Critical Mass

Mackenzie and I had a long talk about how things are going in postretirement life. She was commenting on how far I've come, how excited I seem, how my skin glows. Okay, not that third thing, but the first two definitely.

It's true. I am in such a better place. When I first retired, I was lost. I had no sense of how I would spend my days, where I would find purpose, where the vice president lives. But looking back, I think being lost was just what I needed.

Having unscheduled time, stillness, boredom even, allowed me the space to realize how unhealthy I had become. It allowed me to see how much of my self-image was tied to my job and the illusion of power or control my work gave me. I felt useful, important, and respected at work, and that was okay. I needed the space to realize that usefulness, importance, and respect were important to me, and that I'd have to find other ways to fulfill those needs. But I also needed to be introspective about things I needed to let go. I needed to lose the thrill I took from swooping in and solving problems for other people, the power I felt when I was "in the know" on confidential issues, and the adrenaline I gulped from having a never-ending to-do list.

I needed the stillness to replace those unhealthy habits with calm, gratitude, and service. Being lost after retirement allowed me to see how busying myself was a distraction from the work I really needed to do—to heal traumas, to learn coping skills, to be able to sit in quiet. Being lost allowed me to see that I was relying on alcohol to numb emotions. It allowed space for me to be kinder to myself—to forgive myself for not doing the sort of public service work I hoped, but was unable, to do. It allowed me to find the things that bring me joy—to replace fear with curiosity. And yes, to learn where the vice president lives, because that's something I should definitely fucking know.

But back to Mackenzie. It's so nice to have her in town, not just because of these good conversations but because she says all sorts of things I don't understand and get to learn.

The most recent example: tuned mass dampers. What the hell are those?

A tuned mass damper is a device put in a building (usually a skyscraper) to reduce vibrations (for example, from high winds or earthquakes) and thus improve the building's structural soundness.

My understanding is that the damper is basically a pendulum-type counterweight put in the middle of the building. When the building swings one way, the counterweight swings the other, offsetting the building's movement.

But, you know, I'd be careful about trusting my understanding about all things physics and engineering. What topics can you trust me on? How to handle an unruly employee, basic triathlon stuff maybe, and *The Bachelorette*. Anything else should be eyed (or eared, I suppose) with suspicion.

Color Me Naked
I've been noticing and wondering about various color associations—like why are porno movies sometimes called "blue" movies?

Because back in the day, cheap pornos were shot with bad-quality black-and-white film, which made everything look blue.

Why are Sunday restrictions (e.g., on the sale of cars or liquor) called blue laws? These laws were initially developed to regulate moral behavior. In the 1700s the word "blue" referred to something perceived as rigidly moral, thus why they were pejoratively called blue laws.

Why are prostitution areas called "red light districts"? I know houses of ill repute had red lights, but why red? Because red was a flattering light, so prostitutes in Amsterdam would carry red lanterns as they met the sailors.

I think I need a red lantern.

Be Steel My Heart

It occurred to me that I have no idea what steel is, nor how it's different from iron. I know iron is an element, but what's steel?

Iron is a soft metal. In order to strengthen it, carbon is added (up to 2 percent) to make steel. Additional elements can be added to change the properties (e.g., corrosion resistance or extreme temperature stability), creating alloy steel. If more than 2 percent carbon is in the mix, then the product is considered cast iron.

Wow, who knew? I just thought cast iron was iron that was cast in the shape of a skillet, Dutch oven, or penis-shaped cornbread muffin pan.

Don't Drive Like Your Mother

While Mackenzie is in town, she's been borrowing my car from time to time. She commented that my car has better pickup than normal. She postulated (no kidding, she used that word) it's because I haven't been driving it, so the car has unlearned my ways. What? The? Heck? Is? She? Talking? About?

Mackenzie explained that cars have adaptive gear boxes that learn and respond to the way people drive. She said if I punch the gas when I drive, the car learns it has to take it easy when I do that. Since I'm no longer driving to work every day, perhaps the car has forgotten my bad habits.

Thing one: It's bad form to complain about Mom's driving when you're borrowing her car.

Thing two: Mackenzie is wrong anyway. Adaptive gear boxes do respond to your driving, such as by putting the car in sport mode (which delays upshifts and speeds up downshifts) if you punch the brake or accelerator. But cars do not learn your bad habits. Once you turn off the car, you've got a fresh start with the adaptive gear box learning.

So there.

But hey, I'm noticing a trend. The things Mackenzie says with such certainty are often untrue. I'll be more suspicious going forward.

She is right about some things though, like buffeting.

We were in Clark's car. The air conditioning was acting up, so we had the back window slightly down. The window started making that thump-thump-thump sound that hurts your ears, and I could feel the reverberation down to my toes.

Mackenzie told us the term for that sound is buffeting. How does she know all of the stuff? It's like she's a living Wikipedia, right there in the back seat of the car.

It is also called wind throb, and more technically, Helmholtz resonance. It's the same phenomenon that creates the humming sound when you blow into a bottle.

I tried to look up a Helmholtz Resonance for Dummies explanation so I could explain it to you, but remember how I told you my brain doesn't do science? I can't find an explanation I understand, and I can't bring myself to ask Mackenzie yet again to explain something to her dumb mama. So if you find an explanation you understand, will you school me? But know your audience. I will need a lot of patience, a visual aid, and some way to relate the concept to reality television.

I Gotta Pee

You know how the toilet seats in public restrooms are crescent shaped, but toilet seats in homes are full oval seats without the cutout in front? Why is that? Is the cutout meant to make it easier for guys to hit their mark?

Apparently not. The cutout is intended to make it easier for women to wipe without getting urine on them. *{Hate to be a skeptic, but the politicians were thinking about the women? Really?}* The requirement of open-front toilet seats is found in the International Plumbing Code, which many states pattern their laws on, and provides, in part:

> Water closets shall be equipped with seats of
> smooth, nonabsorbent material. Seats of water
> closets provided for public or employee toilet
> facilities shall be of the hinged open-front type.
> *{I just want to say I am so thankful the law requires*
> *toilet seats be made of nonabsorbent material.}*

There are other benefits to the open-front seat. Because there's less seat, there's less area beneath it where urine can get trapped and thus less cleaning needed. Also, because there's less material used to make the seat, open-front toilet seats are cheaper.

With all of the benefits, why don't we have open-front toilet seats in homes? The best answer I found is that it's custom. Open-front seats look too industrial for home use, and given the lower usage of home toilets, the sanitary benefits of the open front aren't as necessary.

Now I feel so fancy with my full circle toilet seat.

Whip Me

Speaking of politicians (who are doing difficult, difficult work, what with all that focusing on women and their potty needs), what is a whip—not the nine-foot stick kind the circus ringmaster snaps about or the cat-o'-nine-tails they put in bed with the drunken sailor, but the politics kind?

The whip is the disciplinarian of the political party, selected by the party's organizing caucus. Whips are in charge of getting party members in line, assuring they vote the way the party prefers, and making sure they don't go out and get drunk on trashcan punch and miss the vote altogether. *{Whips were named after "whippers in" in fox hunting, the men responsible for making the foxhounds behave. I'm guessing that was an easier job than wrangling politicians.}*

But it's not all stick and no carrot. Whips reward politicians who vote the right way with things like campaign donations, primo committee assignments, and I'm guessing lots and lots of high-grade cocaine.

In both the US House of Representatives and the Senate, the whip of the minority party is outranked only by the minority leader.

The whip of the majority party is the third highest-ranking individual in both the House and the Senate. In the House, the majority whip is outranked by the majority leader and the Speaker. In the Senate, the majority whip is outranked by the majority leader and the president pro tempore.

What's a president pro tempore?

By tradition, the president pro tem is the most senior senator of the majority party. Technically this position presides over the Senate when the vice president is not available. But in reality, the president pro tem delegates this responsibility to junior senators, to give them experience in parliamentary procedure. The president pro tem is third in line of succession to the presidency, behind the vice president and the Speaker of the House.

The End of the Circus

Okay, that was fun, but since I mentioned a ringmaster a bit ago I'm now curious about the circus. Is Ringling Bros. and Barnum & Bailey Circus still a thing? Did I hear they got rid of it? Or did they just get rid of the elephants?

Both. Ringling retired the elephants in May 2016, and in January 2017 they announced they would be doing only thirty more shows. The last show was on May 21, 2017.

That's a bit sad from a nostalgia perspective, but a lot happy from a that-sure-sucked-for-the-animals perspective.

It's fitting that my year of learning should end here, on the entry about ending the whole damn circus.

For quite a while after I quit work, I felt weird about not working. I would stumble when people asked me what I did. This is how every conversation went with someone I had just met.

Someone: "Nice to meet you. What do you do?"

Me: "I'm a lawyer. Not the kind who sues people though. I'm an employment lawyer, so I give advice about human resources stuff. Well, not anymore really. I quit. I'm still a lawyer though. I kept my license. But I'm not working these days. I retired, I guess. I know I seem young for that. Who knows, maybe I'll go back to work someday, but not now. Now I'm enjoying not working. So yeah, I guess I should say I'm retired. Yeah, rewind. Ask me the question again? Because I'd say I'm retired. Because I'm retired."

And the stranger would slowly back away.

I felt a confusing combination of relief that I no longer had to work, guilt that I was so privileged that I could retire young, concern that I wasn't doing anything meaningful, fear that I would spend through all of my money, delight that I didn't have to set an alarm for the morning, joy that I could spend each day however I pleased, and desire to watch all of the TV.

Relief, guilt, concern, fear, delight, joy, and desire. That about covers it.

But now, a year later, all the doubt is gone.

Someone: "Nice to meet you. What do you do?"
Me: "I'm retired."
Someone: "I'm so jealous!" *{At this point in the conversation, my brain is saying, "I think you mean 'envious.'" Sometimes my brain is such an asshole.}*
Me: "Yeah, it's pretty great."

But do I really have no more guilt, concern, or fear? Am I only full of relief, delight, and joy? Pretty much. I'm human, so I do worry some, of course. But then I remind myself I have ways of making my life meaningful. I read and write. I get together with friends. I do some pro bono legal work. And I still watch *Married at First Sight* (yeah, I admitted it).

Basically I'm able to put myself wherever makes sense at that moment, following whatever sense of curiosity or concern brought me there. And that, my friends, is delightful.

!?

All the Curiosity

Now that this exercise in learning is done, what am I taking away? And if you embark upon a project to notice and learn the things you do not know, what do I hope you will take away?

First, there are so many things in this world we don't know. Often we don't even realize we don't know the thing. Faced with an unknown, our brains either decide that thing is unimportant and move right along or they completely fabricate an explanation to satisfy the lack of knowledge.

Eyes: Alert! Alert! I'm reading a word I do not know!
Brain: No problem. Just skim over it. Pretend it's not there.
Eyes: But I think this word might be a critical one.
Brain: Stop overthinking things! I'll make up whatever definition meets my fancy! *{And that's how, dead serious, I spent forty years of my life thinking a manger was a little barn full of Mary, Jesus, and wise men. It's embarrassing how old I was when I learned the manger was actually the trough.}*

Option one leads to a lack of growth and learning. Option two leads to incorrect assumptions. Either is a bad option.

When we pay attention to the things we are curious about, our curiosities lead us to how we can make meaning in our lives, like psychologist Erik Erikson (from the "All the Animals" chapter) told us we must do. I've learned that I am curious about all sorts of things—except history or science, about which I am not at all curious. *{Okay, that's a lie. I'm curious about history and science, just not curious enough to learn about them with any depth. Skim-and-run curious, I'd say.}*

But I'm most drawn to words. I enjoy knowing what they mean and where they come from. I enjoy seeing how they are put together. I appreciate the power they have to change perceptions, to give voice to those marginalized, to make us laugh. For now, I think harnessing the power of words is my purpose.

Working on this curiosity project made me realize how much joy writing gives me. It made me want to study the craft of writing, to discover how to communicate effectively all of the ideas swirling around in my noggin. It spurred me to sign up for a satire writing course with Second City, where I was inspired by the hella funny folks in the class.

Writing humor and satire has given me the space to criticize things I otherwise couldn't. It has given me a way to call attention to problems in our culture in a way that people might actually hear. No, I am not volunteering in the detention centers, lobbying for gun safety, or registering voters; I am addressing these issues in a different way—by using my privilege and platform to give voice to these concerns, and I feel good about that.

Writing is giving me my voice back. Yes, my voice can be loud, opinionated, and profane, but I'm trying not to self-censor. That's the gift of midlife. You get to be yourself without much concern about what others will think. Won't some people be scared away? Most certainly, but I have too many people to keep up with anyway. Besides, those people annoyed the fuck out of me.

I am now actively fighting against becoming stagnant, and I hope you will too. It's easy to spend your days watching *90 Day Fiancé*, but it ain't that fulfilling.

What is fulfilling? Well, that'll be different for you. Maybe you'll want to write a book of your own. Or paint. Or sculpt. Or care for your grandkids. Or run for office. Or. Or. Or. There are so many options.

For me? I've found the most fulfillment in retirement by using humor and satire to call out bullshit—sexism, racism, ageism, ableism, evangelism, footballism, or whatever other fucking ism that needs to be yelled about. I have the privilege to be mouthy, so I don't plan to shut up.

My hope for you, my friends? That you follow your every curiosity. Chase each (legal) thing you are interested in. Find your voice. Then fucking SCREAM.

Acknowledgments

I almost hate to include acknowledgments, because I know there will be many people I will forget to thank. I've decided to name just a few. The rest of you will know, deep in your hearts, that I'm so grateful to you, even though I was kind of a jerk in failing to acknowledge you.

When I decided I wanted to focus on writing, I turned to Second City's writing program. Riane Konc and Brooke Preston were fabulous teachers. And the first readers of chapters of this book were Second City classmates, to whom I am so grateful: Shannon Carpenter, Jen Freymond, Rebekah Iliff, Tomo Lazovich, Dave Liu, Kristen Mulrooney, Rochelle Newman, and Catherine Weingarten.

Elissa Bassist, author of *Hysterical*, was generous to share a copy of her proposal, to shower me with encouragement, and to teach me how things are done. (If you have the opportunity to take one of her classes, do it!)

Allison K. Williams also gave me editorial feedback about the book. And I never, ever would have finished the thing without the ever-patient Claire Linic, who coached me through to the end.

Others along the way encouraged me to keep going: Jeannie Ralston of *NextTribe* (who took me on as a baby humor writer), Andrea Askowitz (who had every conversation there could possibly be had about this book), and so many more.

The Authors Guild and my friend and fellow attorney Michele Martell helped me with the legal end of things.

The book would not exist but for the wonderful team at Trinity University Press. And it got extra eyeballs on it thanks to the great folks at Kaye Publicity.

I've been fortunate to have a writing group who keeps me accountable. Thank you Kate Beeby, Dennis Blackledge, and Shelley Crook, for reading early pages of everything I write. And a shout-out to Kerry Savage, who is making sure this won't be my last book.

For all of my Instagram and other social media pals, thank you for letting me be silly and weird and still hanging around. You're the best.

I would never have shown my face on social media without Ashleigh Renard's coaching. And the social media landscape would have felt a chore without the early assistance of Lauren Petraglia and her team, and now the help of Heather O'Day.

To my mother, my siblings, my kids, and my dear friends, who have had to listen to me talk about this book for *years*, all of my love.

And I save my most profound thanks to all of you reading this book. You are the very best.

I know you're sitting there all like, "What about Rob? Aren't you going to thank Rob?" Well, we split up a while after I finished writing this, so my feelings are complicated. But yes, gratitude is most definitely among them.

LUCIE FROST retired as an employment lawyer and is now a writer. She is a regular contributor to *NextTribe*, and has written for *Slackjaw*, the *Belladonna*, *Points in Case*, and other publications. She lives in San Antonio, Texas, with her three needy, delightful dogs.

www.ingramcontent.com/pod-product-compliance
Lightning Source LLC
Jackson TN
JSHW020924060725
86475JS00002B/2